The Secrets of Troy

TAN Travel Guide

© Copyright 2020 by Izabela Miszczak

Technical editing: J&M

On the cover: Ramp of Troy II

ISBN: 978-83-953130-7-3 (paperback)
ISBN: 978-83-953130-8-0 (Amazon Kindle)
ISBN: 978-83-953130-9-7 (ePub)

Publisher: ASLAN Publishing House

Contact: contact@turkisharchaeonews.net
Facebook: https://facebook.com/turkisharchaeonews
WWW: https://turkisharchaeonews.net/

All rights reserved.

First Edition. January 2020.

Figures and photos copyright: Iza and Jarek Miszczak

Izabela Miszczak

The Secrets of Troy

TAN Travel Guide

Contents

Preface	v
Introduction	1
Trojan War – a myth or a historical fact?	5
History of Troy	9
Archaeological research	19
Sightseeing tour of Troy	25
Troy Museum	63
Bibliography	103
About the Author	105
About Turkish Archaeological News	105

Preface

The tale of mighty Troy has tempted the travellers for thousands of years. The tragic fate of the powerful city of King Priam, sung by the semi-legendary bard called Homer, has been one of the most frequently retold dramas of all times. Even in the ancient times, when Asia Minor was colonised by the Greeks and later controlled by the Romans, the site of Troy was a great tourist attraction. When visiting this World Heritage Site, you will be following in the footsteps of the Persian ruler Xerxes, Alexander the Great of Macedonia, Roman Emperor Hadrian, and the Ottoman Sultan Mehmed II the Conqueror.

Even if it is difficult to say with certainty that the archaeological site first excavated in the 19th century is the location of the Trojan War, the visit here brings many emotions and evokes the scenes from the Homer's story. By following this guidebook, you will be able to imagine brave Achilles chasing the Trojan prince Hector around the mighty fortifications of Troy. The book will also help you to understand the geography of the site and the surrounding countryside. On a bright day, you will see the remote Aegean Islands where the Greek ships had been hidden before the fall of the city. Looking in another direction, you will glimpse the distant outlines of Mount Ida - the favourite location of the Olympian gods who had played with the mythical heroes' fates like a game of chess.

Moreover, this guidebook offers you a tour of the archaeological site that is, admittedly, quite difficult to understand with its multiple layers. All significant locations are described in great detail to add more satisfaction to the experience. Before you come to Troy, make sure to read the chapters devoted to the site's archaeology and history. Finally, the newly opened Troy Museum, located not far from the site, has been thoroughly presented in this book and you might want to visit it before taking a tour of the site.

In this guidebook you will find a detailed plan of the site of Troy, showing all the main stops of the tour. The map of the region of Troad will assist you in putting Troy in the wider geographical context. It should be also helpful during the visit to the Troy Museum where the presented exhibits include not only the objects from Troy, but also from other nearby sites. The book provides practical information for the visitors such as ticket prices and opening hours as well as the transportation options from the city of Çanakkale. If all of this is not enough, there is a bibliography to satisfy the needs of the most inquiring readers.

Introduction

> *Sing, O goddess, the anger of Achilles son of Peleus,*
> *that brought countless ills upon the Achaeans.*
> *Many a brave soul did it send hurrying down to Hades,*
> *and many a hero did it yield a prey to dogs and vultures,*
> *for so were the counsels of Jove fulfilled from the day on*
> *which the son of Atreus,*
> *king of men, and great Achilles, first fell out with one*
> *another.*
> Homer, The Iliad, Book I, translated by Samuel Butler

The tale of Troy, sung by the blind bard Homer, has been retold for almost three thousand years. The story of a mighty and prosperous city, besieged for ten years by the Greek army over the abduction of Helen, the most beautiful woman in the world, is highly dramatic and full of unexpected twists of action. Heroes fight bravely, die tragically, while the Olympian gods play the games with their fates.

This beautifully told mythical story has always been an inspiration for writers, poets, and scriptwriters, from Shakespeare's 'Troilus and Cressida' to Hollywood's blockbuster film 'Troy'. Also, travellers, adventurers, and archaeologists tried to discover the secrets of Troy, thought to be the lost city, for many centuries. Today, it is widely believed that the Homeric Troy had really existed and its location was in Asia Minor, near the shores of the Dardanelles. The inconspicuous hill called Hisarlık is now an active archaeological site, visited by numerous travellers who want to find out more about the place where the mighty Troy fell to the Greeks.

The Secrets of Troy

The visit to Troy offers a unique opportunity to walk in the location where the Trojan prince Hector and the Greek warrior Achilles run around the mighty walls of the city. From the viewing platforms, you can look out into the distant waters of the Dardanelles, just like beautiful Helen gazed out of her window, wondering about the tricks of fate that brought her from her home in Sparta to the distant Anatolian city of Troy.

Hisarlık Hill has an invaluable significance for studying the history of this region of Asia Minor. It provides plentiful sources of information about the development of urban centres in the Bronze Age. The walk around the ruins of Troy is also a valuable lesson about the history of archaeology. Not only can you see with your own eyes the archaeological evidence behind the existence of Troy, but also inspect the results of the latest excavations that are still ongoing.

Moreover, the site of Troy offers excellent insight into the changes in the archaeological methods over the last century. When famous adventurer and amateur archaeologist Heinrich Schliemann excavated Troy at the end of the 19th century, he was so eager to find the dreamed-of Troy described by Homer that he led the excavations in a manner that caused more harm than good. His frantic work destroyed some of the upper layers of the city, including – as it later turned out – the fragments of the settlement that had belonged to Troy of Homer's epic.

The walk around Troy will take you to all the most important discoveries of the area, starting from a modern wooden replica of the Trojan Horse. It commemorates the trick employed by the Greeks who were tired of besieging Troy for a decade. Cunning Odysseus, the king of Ithaca, suggested building an enormous wooden horse. The elite of warriors hid inside it, while the other Greeks pretended to sail away. The jubilant Trojans wheeled the horse into their city and started the celebrations. When the night fell, the Greeks sneaked out of the horse under cover of darkness and opened the gates of Troy. The Greek army entered the city, destroyed it, and killed its inhabitants.

Introduction

As you continue the walk, you will also encounter the massive fortifications and towers of the Homeric Troy. At this location, it is possible to see the distant outline of Mount Ida. On this mountain, the Trojan prince Paris was herding his cattle when he was approached by three goddesses: Hera, Athena, and Aphrodite, who asked him to decide which one of them was the most beautiful. Aphrodite won the first-ever beauty contest by promising Paris the love of the most beautiful woman on Earth, Helen of Sparta.

The ruins of the Temple of Athena are another fascinating place to visit in Troy. It is hard to believe that these humble remains are all that is left of the magnificent building where Alexander the Great on sacrificed to Athena and poured libations to the heroes. He also promised to construct a new temple and donated his armour to the goddess.

Off the beaten track you can also see the mysterious Water Cave of Wilusa. To get there, you should follow a narrow path through the meadows and fields, pleasantly shaded by many trees. On the way, it is possible to imagine that you are walking in the place where the Greek warriors were camping during the siege of Troy. The cave is an artificial structure, carved deep into the rock. There is a fascinating connection between this cave, the Hittite documents, and the Homeric Troy. The historical inscription called the Wilusa Treaty mentioned the vassal monarch of the Hittites, Alaksandu. This name is sometimes interpreted as a distortion of the Greek name Alexandros, and as such, it would provide the link to the legend of the Trojan War as Paris of Troy was also known as Alexandros of Ilios.

The visit to Troy will significantly improve the understanding of this site, its development over time, and the role it played in the ancient world. From an archaeological point of view, the site has a long history, fascinating in its own rights and standing apart from the legend of the Trojan War. However, the song of Homer and the site are inextricably connected. There are not many travellers who can stand on the mighty walls of the windy Troy and not imagine the enormous Greek army gathered below, ready to attack.

The Secrets of Troy

Trojan War – a myth or a historical fact?

The history of the Trojan War, or actually its final phase, was presented in the Iliad created by the ancient bard Homer. It is not known precisely when this epic poem was composed. Some people believe that it happened shortly after the war, which was supposedly fought in the 12th century BCE, while others, including Herodotus, suggest the 9th century BCE.

Almost everyone knows the cause of the outbreak of the Trojan War. As a reminder, it all started because of a woman, the most beautiful one – Helen, wife of Menelaus. The prince of Trojans – Paris – won her thanks to the favourable judgement for Aphrodite, the Greek goddess of love, in the first-ever beauty contest. Paris abducted Helen from Mycenae and brought to Troy, to the castle ruled by his father, king Priam.

The abduction of beautiful Helen greatly upset the Greeks, even more so as her husband Menelaus was a legitimate brother of Agamemnon, the king of Mycenae. Greek troops crossed the Aegean Sea and besieged Troy for ten years. In the end, the city fell, mainly due to the trick of Odysseus, who came up with the idea of constructing a wooden horse. The bravest Greek warriors hid in this bizarre structure, and the remaining troops pretended to withdraw. Jubilant residents of Troy took the horse inside the city and began to celebrate the end of a devastating war. Then, under the cover of night, Odysseus and his companions opened the gates of the city, letting the Greek army in. The slaughter began, followed by complete collapse and burning of Troy.

However, the identification of the ruins located on Hisarlık Hill with the legendary Troy has long been questioned. The researchers do not consider the events described in the Iliad as a description of the actual history of the city. It is thought that the epic is a compilation of traditions, myths, and stories handed down from generation to generation, concerning different historical events, distorted by time and the ephemeral human memory.

Descriptions left by Homer leave no doubt as to the fact that the Trojan War had been fought in the Troad region, near the Dardanelles. Researchers have long tried to reconcile the poetic vision presented in the Iliad with the historical events that occurred in the Late Bronze Age in the Troad. Clay tablets, discovered in the capital of the Hittites – Hattusa – provide two names that may be the missing link in this history. The first name is Wilusa, the land in the north-western Anatolia, whose capital could be Troy. The second name is Ahhiyawa, meaning most likely Mycenae – if we remember that the Greeks called themselves the Achaeans. The memory of the ongoing conflicts between Wilusa and Mycenae during the restless period of the late second millennium BCE may have survived as the story of the Trojan War.

On the other hand, the archaeological work carried out in the territory of Troy has not provided any convincing evidence that the invaders from Greece destroyed the city. It is known, however, that a settlement on Hisarlık Hill was then an important regional centre, well-fortified and consistently rebuilt after subsequent devastations caused by fires, earthquakes, and wars.

In the course of the archaeological work in the area of the settlement, the researchers tried to link individual layers to the Homeric Troy. Heinrich Schliemann was convinced that the burned citadel belonging to Troy II and its so-called Treasure of Priam constituted sufficient proof of the truth of the story presented in the Iliad. However, subsequent studies have shown that Troy II was more than a millennium older than the Mycenaean civilization. Dörpfeld, who was responsible for excavations of the Late Bronze Age settlement, argued that proper identification of Homeric Troy points to Troy VI, but Blegen undermined his argument. This researcher argued that small buildings and food storages from Troy

VIIa indicate precisely that this layer was a city besieged by the army from Greece. We now know, however, that at the same time, there was an extensive settlement outside the city walls, and the interpretation of traces of fire and several human bones as a proof of the waged war is highly controversial.

No matter if the famous Trojan War was fought in the area, Hisarlık Hill has an invaluable significance for studying the history of this region of Asia Minor. It provides plentiful sources of information about the development of urban centres in the Bronze Age. However, Homer's work has played an essential role in culture and art for many centuries. The visitors of the ruins of Troy on Hisarlık Hill follow in the footsteps of great historical figures. This location was visited both by the Persian ruler Xerxes and Alexander the Great of Macedonia, as well as many Roman emperors and Ottoman Sultan Mehmed II the Conqueror. When this sultan arrived at the ruined citadel in 1462, the site had been abandoned for around a millennium. Mehmed II regarded the Trojan warriors as his kinsmen as his speech made during the visit emphasized his conquest of Constantinople as the vengeance for the Trojans' defeat by the Greeks. Even the landing of Allied troops on the Gallipoli Peninsula in 1915 was presented as a 'new Trojan War.' This shows just how significant and memorable were the events of this legendary military conflict.

The Secrets of Troy

History of Troy

Troy is located on a 15-meter-high hill that hides the traces of the successive waves of colonization. Although once it lay near the coast, now, as a result of the alluvial activity of Scamander River (now called Karamenderes), it is 5 km away from the sea. The location of the ancient settlement – on the coast, on the border of two continents, and at the intersection of trade routes from Asia Minor to the Balkans and the Aegean and the Black Sea – was crucial to the development and prosperity of its people. In order to systematize the history of Troy, archaeologists divided it into nine historical periods, corresponding to the successive layers of settlements, which in turn often are divided into subperiods.

The history of the city dates back to the Early Bronze Age, i.e. around the year 3000 BCE, when the first settlement, marked now as Troy I (2920-2550 BCE), was most probably established here. It was a small village, built on terraces on the coast, consisting of interconnected stone and brick houses. The settlement was surrounded by stone walls, repeatedly strengthened. The objects found in one of the houses suggest that it could belong to a local ruler. This dwelling had a large hearth in the centre and a smaller one at the back. Moreover, infant burials were uncovered inside jars placed under the floor of the building.

This settlement had many common features with other villages located on the shore of the Aegean Sea and the Sea of Marmara as well as on the nearby islands. The items found in the earliest layers are mostly dark, hand-produced ceramics, and copper objects. Today, you can admire the restored gate to the village, and one of the houses.

The Secrets of Troy

Troy II (2550-2250 BCE) consists of 7 layers lying one on the other. Each of them was surrounded by city walls, and a monumental ceremonial gate led into the interior of the town. The settlement from this period was twice destroyed by fire. In addition, at this time, the first buildings were erected outside the ramparts, gradually creating a vast settlement surrounded by a palisade. This Lower City was discovered relatively recently.

Archaeological finds from this period include yellow-reddish ceramics produced using a potter's wheel, as indicated by their symmetrical, almost identical shapes. The most distinctive pottery from this period is the tall drinking vessel with double handles, called the Depas Amphikypellon. Also, numerous jewellery pieces were found in this layer, made of silver, gold, and amber. Moreover, so-called Priam's Treasure found by Schliemann has been dated to this period of Troy history.

The ceramics from Troy III (2250-2200 BCE) are virtually indistinguishable from the vessels of Troy II. A fascinating find from Troy III was uncovered in the excavation period of 1998-1999. It is a megaron, i.e. a building with an antechamber, erected of mud-brick walls on stone foundations.

The three earliest periods of Troy – I, II, and III – are defined by archaeologists as the Trojan Maritime Culture. Not much is known about the identity and language of the first Trojans. However, we know that their basic diet depended on agriculture, animal husbandry, and fishing. They ate cattle, fallow deer, goat, lamb, wild birds, fish, and other seafood. Their menu also included peas, lentils, grapes, olives, figs, and cereals such as barley, einkorn, and emmer. The Trojan mound was surrounded by arable land, extending to the diameter of two kilometres.

These early Trojans prepared and cooked food in their own houses, by placing tripod vessels over a fire. Their hand-made pottery had a dark brown-black colour with partial white decoration. Their houses, of the so-called megaron type, were very similar to the ones found in other, contemporaneous settlements of Asia Minor, including Elmalı near Antalya and Beycesultan near Çivril.

History of Troy

On the basis of small idols depicting the female body, archaeologists have suggested that fertility cults played a significant role in the lives of these Trojans.

Troy IV and V (2200-1750 BCE) represent the period of the gradual development of the city. As Troy III was destroyed in a fire or by an earthquake, professor Korfmann proposed that the new settlers who arrived at Troy could have been of Anatolian origins. This suggestion has been based on the methods they used to erect houses and produce pottery. Therefore, the archaeologists have dubbed this period the Anatolian Trojan Culture.

We have relatively little information about this stage of the existence of Troy. The scarcity of information results from the progress of the archaeological work, and the severe damage done by Schliemann, who dug through these layers in search of Homeric Troy, irretrievably damaging the chronology of the layers. These Trojans lived in larger houses built side by side. Moreover, more decorative thin-walled vessels were made on a faster wheel. The grave findings from these layers indicate the existence of trade relations between Troy and the early Greek city-states, including Mycenae, Crete, the Cyclades, and Cyprus.

Troy VI (1750-1300 BCE) and Troy VIIa (1300-1180 BCE) represent the peak phase of the prosperity of the city in the Late Bronze Age and as such are called the High Trojan Culture period. This is evidenced by the remains of fortifications, far exceeding the previous city walls both in terms of size and quality. However, also in the case of these layers, the possibility of a thorough examination is severely limited, because the centre of the settlement was destroyed during the levelling of the land for the construction of the Temple of Athena in the Hellenistic period. Moreover, a part of this layer was dug by Schliemann without conducting proper documentation.

The finds from Troy VI and VIIa, mostly grey ceramics, testify to the strong ties with the Greek civilization. Several vessels imported from Crete, Mycenae, Cyprus, and the Levant have also been found. However, despite Troy's apparent wealth and power, it was not the dominant state of Asia Minor in the Late Bronze Age. The Hittite Empire controlled most of Anatolia in that period, and the Hittites formed alliances with smaller kingdoms situated to the west and south of their domains. These kingdoms were, for instance, the Seha River Land, Mira in Ionia, and Wilusa as Troy was then referred to. All these kingdoms used the Luvian language.

At the same time, the Myceneans also tried to establish a foothold in Asia Minor, and they founded a colony called Millawanda, now better-known as classical Miletus. The Myceneans were referred to as the Ahhiyawans (Achaeans) by the Hittites, and these two entities were engaged in continuous power struggles along the western coast of Asia Minor. This conflict lasted for about two centuries, from around 1400 to 1200 BCE. In the 1280s, the Hittite King Muwattali III and the Trojan/Wilusan King Alaksandu concluded a treaty that brought Wilusa within the Hittite sphere of influence against the increasing power of the Myceneans. Thus, Wilusa effectively became a vassal state of the Hittites, and as such, it was required to support them with troops and chariots during military conflicts.

These challenging and dangerous times were reflected in the changes to the architecture of the city. During this period the city was surrounded by massive walls, encompassing the inner area of 2 hectares. These walls were 5 meters wide and 10 meters high. Defensive ramparts and bastions were continually strengthened, and new towers were erected. Moreover, the western gate, facing the Trojan Plain and the harbour was blocked. Inside, there were large detached two-storey buildings, 35 meters long, situated along cobbled streets. The method of their construction – with stone blocks and no windows on the ground floor - can attest to their defensive character.

Apart from the buildings inside the citadel, the so-called Lower City developed outside the city walls, with houses, workshops, and streets. It was surrounded by two moats, of which the inner one demarcated an area of 30 hectares, and the outer one – an even more extensive area. These defensive ditches were dug out of bedrock, possibly to prevent war chariots from attacking the settlement.

The buildings belonging to Troy VIIa had a different appearance than the palaces of Troy VI as they were smaller and had well-stocked pantries in the form of massive vessels buried in the floor. Their different nature is the evidence of social change. In the period of Troy VI, its residents began to use horses for the first time. Horse-breeding, food supply, and trade were controlled by the rulers of Troy who dwelled in the palaces within the citadel.

Both layers – VI and VIIa – were rapidly destroyed, for unknown reasons. The destruction is evidenced by the fallen stone blocks and the traces of fire. The hypothesis put forward by Blegen states that these are the traces of an earthquake, but not all researchers agree with this theory.

The destruction of Troy VIIa was simultaneous with the collapse of the Bronze Age kingdoms of the Mediterranean that occurred around 1200 BCE. Hittite and Mycenean palaces, once so powerful, fell one by one, and the prosperous harbour cities of the Levant gradually disappeared. This difficult period of history is often called the beginning of the Dark Ages and associated with the influx of the invaders referred to as the Sea Peoples, mentioned in the contemporary Egyptian sources.

Researchers do not agree on what exactly happened. Still, one thing is sure: during the 12th century, the once flourishing areas of Asia Minor, Greece, and the Levant were torn apart as the result of the combination of raids, migrations, social unrest, and the climate change. The destruction of Troy around 1180 BCE has been for a long time connected with the events of the legendary Trojan War.

The period between 1100 and 800 BCE is often described as the Dark Ages because writing disappeared in the Aegean region, and the populations were decreased in size. Also, the trade did not flourish as it had before. Moreover, as bronze was replaced by iron, Anatolia entered the Iron Age.

The Secrets of Troy

Troy VIIb (1180-950 BCE) was established on the ruins of Troy VIIa. The destruction of the mighty Hittite Empire brought chaos in Asia Minor. While the surviving Hittite princes moved to southeastern Anatolia, the western part of Asia Minor absorbed immigrants from other regions. The newly arrived people from the area of the Balkans settled in Phrygia but also around Troy. The houses inside and outside the citadel were rebuilt and fortified, and the wall was repaired.

The finds from this period, including Protogeometric ceramics, testify to the transition to the Iron Age settlement. The new, distinctive style is characterised by decorative elements such as concentric circles, triangles, and wavy lines. The existence of such ceramics at Troy testifies to the renewed trade contacts with Greece. Some of the vessels found at Troy were imported while others were locally-made imitations. The end of this settlement came with another fire, traces of which are visible on some buildings.

In the period between Troy VIIb and Troy VIII (950-700 BCE), no traces of settlements have been identified, which means that at that time the hill was uninhabited, or it was only a very insignificant village.

Amazingly, in this apparently dark period of the city's history, the most critical event that immortalised Troy took place. In the late 8th century, the great Greek bard Homer recorded the story of the war that had supposedly been fought in Troy half a millennium earlier.

Homer's war stories were later sung and repeated by professional artists known as the rhapsodes who performed during ceremonies and feasts. The tale of the Trojan War referred to as the Iliad quickly spread and became extremely popular in the ancient world. The story was known in ancient Phrygia ruled by King Midas, in the Lydian Kingdom with its capital at Sardis, and, most importantly, in the Greek colonies of the Aegean coast.

This immense popularity of the Iliad was not without the significance to the settlement of Troy itself. The city of the Greek and Roman periods became a tourism centre, with many prominent historical figures visiting to see the place where the Trojan War had taken place. Troy VIII (about 700-85 BCE) was known as Ilion. It was the settlement of the Greeks who restored the city. The first temples and altars were erected in the Archaic style. In 480 BCE, when the Achaemenid king Xerxes embarked on a campaign against Greece, he made sacrifices in the temple of Troy. The Spartan commander Mindarus did the same in 411 BCE.

In 334 BCE, Alexander of Macedonia visited Ilion and also made sacrifices. He even had decided to build a new Temple of Athena in the city, but this plan was only executed later, by his successors. The Hellenistic period was the beginning of a whole new era for Troy as it became a full-blown city again: with a bouleuterion and a theatre. Around 310 BCE, Ilion was also a central hub for a confederation of the cities of the Troad, by the decision of Antigonus, one of the commanders of Alexander the Great. This league was centred on the Sanctuary of Athena at Ilion and consisted of at least twenty cities.

Around the mid-3rd century BCE, the fortifications of Troy were renovated. At the same time, the Greek inhabitants commemorated their city's distant past as the ancient burial mounds were restored. The city was not destroyed when the Galatians invaded Asia Minor in 217 BCE, but this was, most possibly, due to the diplomatic efforts, and not because of the mighty fortifications. The tourists who visited Ilion in the 2nd century BCE included such figures as the Seleucid king Antiochus III the Great, Gaius Livius Salinator, and Lucius Cornelius Scipio.

In the 80s of the first century BCE, Rome waged war in Asia Minor against the ruler of Pontus, king Mithridates VI. Many Greek cities, including Ilion, granted their support to Mithridates, and were severely punished after his defeat. In 85 BCE, Ilion was ravaged by a Roman leader called Gaius Flavius Fimbria, who was famous for his exceptional ruthlessness. However, the symbolic importance of Troy was too significant to let the city fall into ruin. Many Roman leaders such as Sulla and Caesar made promises to restore Troy, but the process was gradual.

Troy IX (85 BCE - 500 CE), which was soon rebuilt on the ruins of Troy VIII, was called Ilium. It was a Hellenistic-Roman city, and the most exciting findings of this layer are an odeon and a bouleuterion. The development and prosperity of the city resulted, among other things, from the cherished belief about the relation of Ilium with the mythical Troy. After all, Roman emperors, especially from the Julio-Claudian dynasty, willingly traced their descent from the Trojan royal family and the legendary hero Aeneas of Troy.

The later emperors also remembered about Troy. Hadrian came to the city in 124 CE, and this visit marked the beginning of a new golden era of Troy. He ordered many repairs and had many new buildings constructed, including baths, a nymphaeum, and an aqueduct.

The visit of Emperor Caracalla in 214 CE was not without an accident. The detailed account of this scandalous event was described by Herodian, a Greek historian of the late second and the first half of the third century:

> *He visited all the ruins of that city, coming last to the tomb of Achilles; he adorned this tomb lavishly with garlands of flowers, and immediately he became Achilles. Casting about for a Patroclus, he found one ready to hand in Festus, his favourite freedman, keeper of the emperor's daily record book. This Festus died at Troy; some say he was poisoned so that he could be buried as Patroclus, but others say he died of the disease. Caracalla ordered a huge pyre of logs to be erected and the body of Festus placed in the centre. After sacrificing animals of all kinds, the emperor set fire to the funeral pile; then, taking a bowl and pouring a libation, he offered prayers to the winds. Since he was almost entirely bald, he made himself ridiculous when he wished to place his curls upon the blaze; he did, however, shear off what little hair he had.*
> Herodian of Antioch, History of the Roman Empire, Book 4, translated by Edward C. Echols

Troy survived the attacks of the Goths in 267 CE and recovered

History of Troy

for the final time, possibly sponsored by Emperor Constantine the Great. Two major earthquakes around 500 CE put the end to the city's prosperity. After the fall of the Western Roman Empire, a small Byzantine-period settlement existed on the top of the mound in the 13th century, and it is sometimes referred to as Troy X. Gradually, it fell into disrepair and was forgotten. With time, people ceased to believe in Troy's existence, and the story of the Trojan War has been preserved only in the form of the Homer's epic poem.

The Secrets of Troy

Archaeological research

The tale of a great city of Troy, plunged into a decade of war over the abduction of the most beautiful woman in the world, has always been seen as irresistibly dramatic and inspiring. Its allure has sent pilgrims, adventurers, and archaeologists in search of the city, once believed to have vanished from the surface of the world. For centuries, travellers headed to the Troad, as it has never been doubted that Troy was located in this region, to stand on the ground where the Homeric heroes once valiantly fought and bravely died. However, only the discoveries made in the second half of the 19th century revealed the existence of the ancient city, dating back to the Bronze Age.

In 1793, a cartographer Franz Kauffer first recorded the existence of the mound called Hisarlık on the map prepared for Auguste de Choiseul-Gouffier's book 'Voyage Pittoresque en Grèce'. Moreover, as early as 1822, Hisarlık was identified as a possible site of Homeric Troy by Charles Maclaren, a Scottish journalist and geologist.

In 1847, Frederick Calvert, from the influential British family of diplomats and businessmen, bought a farm which included part of Hisarlık, and this turned out to be a momentous acquisition. His younger brother, Frank Calvert, was convinced that this was the site of the ancient city of Troy. The first archaeological excavations at Hisarlık were conducted in 1856 by an officer of the British Navy – John Burton, and his work was continued in the years 1863-1865 by Frank Calvert. However, he never reached the remains of the Bronze Age city.

When Heinrich Schliemann arrived at Asia Minor in 1870, the

site commonly believed to be Troy was at Pınarbaşı, a hilltop at the south end of the Trojan Plain and this is where Schliemann performed the first excavations. Schliemann excavated at Pınarbaşı because of the confusing information provided by the ancient geographer Strabo. He claimed that the mythical Troy and the city of Ilion that existed in his days were two entirely different cities. In the 19th century, many scholars pointed to Pınarbaşı village, located about 10 km south of Hisarlık, as the most likely location of Troy.

Schliemann's very modest finds at this location were very disappointing, and he was about to abandon the further search. In the last moment, Calvert pointed out the site of Hisarlık to Schliemann during a chance meeting in Çanakkale. Schliemann had a significantly larger budget than Calvert and quickly made tremendous progress at Hisarlık.

Schliemann acquired necessary permits to conduct research, and from 1871 until his death he repeatedly returned to Hisarlık, where he excavated the mysterious mound. Thus, the notion that Schliemann was the discoverer of Troy, the place where the Trojan War had been fought, is the result of an intensive promotional campaign conducted by Schliemann himself. Relatively unknown Frank Calvert died in 1908 and was buried at the English Cemetery in Çanakkale.

Schliemann, eager to find the dreamed-of Troy described by Homer, led the excavations in a manner that caused more harm than good. His work destroyed some of the upper layers of the city, including - as it later turned out - the fragments the settlement that had belonged to Troy of Homer's epic.

In 1873, one of the most sensational discoveries was made by Schliemann. He found a rich collection of objects, consisting of copper pots, bronze weapons and, what was most important to him, silver and gold jewellery. Schliemann announced to the world that he had found the so-called King Priam's treasure, and the magnificent gold necklaces and earrings had once belonged to the beautiful mythical Helen. In fact, as demonstrated by the dating of the layers of Troy, carried out later by Carl Blegen, these items were much older. Finally, they were assigned to Troy II (i.e. to the middle of the third millennium BCE), which existed 1,200 years before the destruction of 'Homeric' Troy.

Schliemann secretly took away the rich collection of finds from Asia Minor. The scientific world and the Ottoman authorities learned about this fact when his wife – Sophia – began to show up in antique jewellery in public. Schliemann lost permission to conduct excavations in Troy. He recovered it later in exchange for the return of a part of the treasure.

Some items of the treasure are now in the collections of the Archaeological Museum in Istanbul. However, the most outstanding exhibits were taken to Germany, where they remained in the Royal Museum in Berlin until 1945. In this year, the collection disappeared in the mysterious circumstances. It was only in 1993 when it reappeared in the Pushkin Museum in Moscow.

Russia keeps the Priam's Treasure as compensation for the destruction of Russian cities and looting of Russian museums by Nazi Germany in the Second World War. Moreover, from the year 1998, Russian law legalizes the looting in Germany as compensation and prevents Russian authorities from proceeding to restitutions. Thus, despite, multiple efforts made for the return of the treasure, undertaken both by the German and the Turkish authorities, the artefacts remain in Moscow.

The excavations at Hisarlık were continued by Wilhelm Dörpfeld – German archaeologist and architect, in the years 1893-1894. He had begun the adventure with Troy earlier, in 1882, as an assistant of Schliemann. After Schliemann's death, as the manager of excavations, Dörpfeld corrected many erroneous conclusions of his former supervisor.

After a break of almost 40 years, archaeological work at Hisarlık resumed in 1932, under the leadership of an American archaeologist Carl Blegen and his team from the University of Cincinnati. During the excavations that continued until 1938, it was established that Troy could be divided into nine main layers corresponding to the cities that existed in this location for many millennia. Blegen even proposed their further subdivision into 46 levels.

Another break in the archaeological work lasted until 1988, when Professor Manfred Korfmann, also of the University of Cincinnati, became the director of Troy excavations. At the same time, Professor Charles Brian Rose was responsible for the study of the youngest layers of the city – Greek, Roman, and Byzantine.

Manfred Korfmann devoted 17 years of his life to the study of Troy. The greatest discovery made while Korfmann was responsible for the Trojan excavations, is the determination that Troy was much bigger than it had been initially thought. In addition to the location on Hisarlık mound, the ancient city covered a wide area around it. Another sensational discovery is associated with the signs of a fight in the city, in the form of bronze arrowheads and human remains, dating to the beginning of the 12th century BCE. These items ignited the imagination of many people and restarted a heated debate on the authenticity of the events known as the Trojan War.

Because of Korfmann's activities, the interest in Troy on the international arena increased significantly. In 1996, he assisted Turkish authorities to establish a National Park covering the areas adjacent to Troy. Two years later, Troy became a UNESCO World Heritage Site. A year before his sudden death in 2005, Korfmann received Turkish citizenship as a token of gratitude for his achievements. He also adopted a middle name – Osman – officially, as for many years he had been known as Osman Bey. After his death, a library bearing his name, containing his collection of books, publications, and documents was opened in the nearby city of Çanakkale.

A team led by Ernst Pernicka of the University of Tübingen continued Korfmann's work from 2006. However, in recent years, the excavations at Troy became the subject of a dispute. In 2013, an interdisciplinary team of researchers, led by William Aylward of the University of Wisconsin, with the patronage of the University of Çanakkale, was supposed to start working in Troy. However, a few days before the beginning of the expedition, the Turkish authorities withdrew the permissions to conduct the excavations for a hundred participants, including the director.

In March 2014, it was announced that new research was planned at Troy, sponsored by a private company and directed by the University of Çanakkale. This was the first team led under the Turkish management to work at Troy, and Professor Rüstem Aslan was appointed as its director. The international team under Rüstem Aslan has been excavating Troy for several years now, and many fascinating finds have been recently reported. For instance, in September of 2019, Professor Aslan announced that new discoveries from excavations at Troy suggest the area may have been used as a settlement more than six centuries earlier than previously known. He explained that the archaeologists came across a new layer which they decided to call Troy 0. If confirmed, this discovery may revolutionise the traditional dating to the layers of Troy, from I to IX.

The Secrets of Troy

Sightseeing tour of Troy

Visiting Troy is a challenging task, even for hardy travellers who have already seen many ancient ruins. Many people are confused by a multitude of layers of the settlement on the hill, and the effects of intensive archaeological work. Fortunately, the area open to the public has an excellent infrastructure, which consists of marked paths, platforms, viewpoints, and information boards. The sightseeing route is well-marked by signposts, and leads the visitors along a loop, returning to the starting point – the Trojan Horse model.

Trojan Horse

Go through the entrance to the archaeological site of Troy, situated next to the ticket office. The main sightseeing route goes straight on, but you can see the model of the Trojan Horse standing on a square, slightly to your right. This modern wooden replica of the Trojan Horse was created in 1975 by the Turkish architect İzzet Senemoğlu. It is possible to get inside the horse and climb up to its two levels. There are windows on both of them, offering an overview of the site.

At the square, there is also a toilet, the only one at the whole site, as well as the official museum shop where you can buy souvenirs, maps, and books devoted to Troy and other archaeological sites in Turkey.

The tale of the Trojan Horse is one of the most frequently told stories from the mythical Trojan War. It tells about the trick employed by the Greeks who were tired of besieging Troy for a decade. Cunning Odysseus, the legendary king of Ithaca, suggested

Trojan Horse

building an enormous wooden horse. When the construction was ready, the elite of warriors hid inside, while the remaining Greeks pretended to sail away, bored of the war. The jubilant Trojans wheeled the horse into the city and started the celebrations. Undercover of the night, the Greeks sneaked out of the horse, opened the gates of Troy, and the Greek army entered the city, destroyed it, and killed its inhabitants.

The fundamental question arises after hearing the tale of the Trojan horse: why would the Greeks build a model of this animal and not another? There are many interpretations of the story. The most straightforward explanation is that the horse was the emblem of Troy, so the Trojans willingly accepted such a gift.

Another speculation states that the horse was a battering ram, such as used at the time by the armies. These devices were covered with wet horse hides to protect them from fire. The horse could also be a ship with the hidden warriors, as ships were called seahorses, for instance in the Odyssey.

Finally, a more complicated theory states that the Trojan Horse

Sightseeing tour of Troy

did not exist in any material form but was a metaphor for an earthquake that destroyed the walls of Troy, letting the Greeks inside. This speculation is supported by the fact that Poseidon was not only the god of the seas but of earthquakes and horses too.

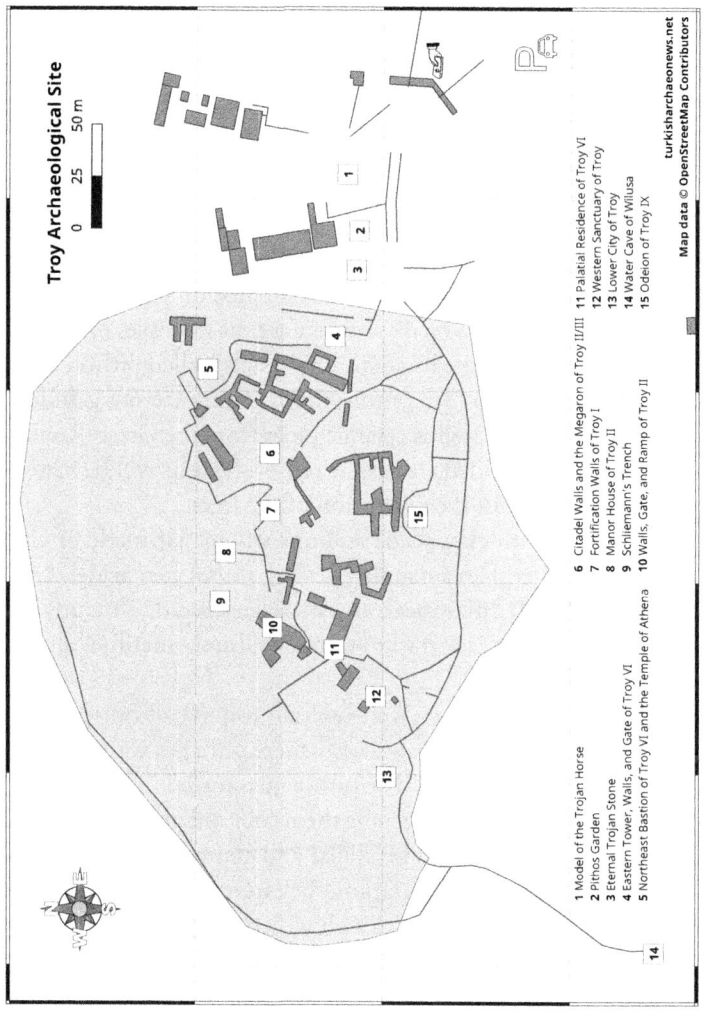

Sightseeing tour of Troy

The Secrets of Troy

The model of the Trojan Horse, 12.5 meters high, was built of 25 cubic meters of pinewood, brought from the Kaz Mountain. This mountain, in ancient times known as Mount Ida, is situated some 50 km to the south-east of Troy. It was the setting of several important episodes of the Trojan War. It was also the place where the Olympian gods sat and watched the progress of the epic fight. Another model of the Trojan Horse, used in the filming of the movie 'Troy' from 2004, stands on the quay in the city of Çanakkale, the main base for the tours of Troy.

Pithos Garden

Walk back from the square to the fork off near the entrance to the site. This time, follow the main sightseeing path, straight on. After walking about 50 meters, you will reach the small outdoor exhibition area, called the Pithos Garden, situated on your right. The archaeological artefacts on display here are the examples of ancient ceramics, including the huge storage vessels, called pithoi, from the period of 15th to 13th century BCE. There are also grinding stones and pestles as well as ceramic pipes from the Greco-Roman times. Enjoy the shaded area as the rest of the tour will be mainly in the open, without the protection of the trees.

A pithos is a thick-walled, bulbous storage jar made of clay, sometimes higher than a standing person. Pithoi were widely used in the ancient Mediterranean and Near East regions, mainly for the storage and transportation of goods, but sometimes also as coffins.

These storage containers were typically found half-buried in the floors of pantries and warehouses, where olive oil, water, honey, salt, and cereals were kept. The pithoi guaranteed the best conditions for these foodstuffs, keeping them cool and protected against rodents. They could also be sealed and stamped to mark their owners. If used for transportation, they were equipped with large handles in the upper part, through which the ropes were pulled. The pithoi shown in the exhibition were found at Troy, for instance in Megaron VI.

Other objects related to food, displayed in the Pithos Garden,

Sightseeing tour of Troy

Pithos Garden

are grinding stones and pestles. These items give us valuable hints about the diet of the ancient Trojans. The cereals have been the basis of the human diet even before the hunter-gatherers settled and domesticated wheat. However, with the development of farming villages, such as the earliest Troy had been, the grains became the staple food.

The fertile Trojan Plain provided excellent farming conditions, but the grain also had to be processed into flour. Practically every household had a grindstone and a hand-held pestle. The monotonous activity of pulverizing the grains was one of the main tasks of girls and women of antiquity, as evidenced in the alternations in the joints of female skeletons.

The ceramic water pipes displayed here are from the newest layers of Troy settlement, representing the Roman period when the city was known as Ilium. The running water was of great importance to the residents of Troy, and these clay pipes indicate that they also understood the recommendations of the architect Vitruvius. He listed three ways for channelling water: stone conduits, lead pipes, and clay pipes. Of these three, he advised to used the clay ones, as cheaper, easier to make, and, most importantly, healthier.

Ilium also benefited from the existence of public baths, once adorned with beautiful mosaics of coloured stones, that were supplied by these pipes. The water came from the nearby hills to the east of the city where some parts of the aqueduct are still standing.

ETERNAL STONE OF TROY

Just beyond the Pithos Garden, also on the right side of the main sightseeing path, there is a small square. Its main attraction is a monumental stone block, called the Eternal Stone of Troy. It is a symbolic monument brought to Troy in 2002, funded by a private sponsor. It commemorates the most important people from the past who contributed to the development of the ancient Troy and its modern-era excavations. After this point, you will start the walk around the hill where the layers of Troy settlement have been unearthed.

The Eternal Stone of Troy is not a relic from the excavations of Troy, but a symbolic block of granite, weighing 20 tons. It is a gift from a local businessman, Süleyman Bodur, who offered this monument to the Troy Foundation in 2002. He is a member of the Friends of Troy, the association created by the people fascinated with the history and archaeology of this ancient city.

The members of the society support the research of Troy, and in some years their financial contribution reaches 10% of the excavation budget. Çanakkale-Tübingen Troy Foundation was established by professor Manfred Korfmann to support the research and preservation of Troy. The Eternal Stone of Troy has an inscription listing the most important sponsors of the city, starting, quite surprisingly with Xerxes, Alexander the Great, and Octavian Augustus.

The Eternal Stone of Troy was erected to attract the visitor's attention to the fact that Troy was one of the first locations on the border of Europe and Asia where dressed stone masonry of smooth rectangular blocks was employed.

You will see examples of this ancient construction technology during the tour of the site, including the vestibule of Megaron of Troy II/III, the earliest instance of its application. Other cases of

Sightseeing tour of Troy

Eternal Stone

using well-hewn stones are visible in the fortifications, residences, and palaces of Troy VI and VII. The excellence of the Trojan architects is confirmed by the fact that these huge, carefully wrought blocks were fitted together without cement and they matched so closely that the interstices between them are hardly visible.

Eastern Fortifications of Troy VI

After the Eternal Stone of Troy, the sightseeing route turns right and leads to the fortifications from the times of Troy VI. These fortifications, possibly of the Homeric city, include the long stretch of walls of ashlar masonry, the ingeniously designed gate, and the magnificent Eastern Tower. The walls were erected around 1700 BCE while the tower was added in the later period, possibly in the 13th century.

Before you go down the stairs and walk along these walls, stop on the viewing platform above. The platform sits on the remains of the wall of the Temple District from the Greek and Roman periods. The traces of the lower city of Greco-Roman Ilion are behind you. In front, you can see a panoramic view of Troy on the Hisarlık Mound and the surrounding countryside.

The Secrets of Troy

Eastern Fortifications of Troy VI

Stay on the platform for a while, to gain some orientation in the geography of the region. In front of you, to the north, on bright days, it is possible to glimpse the waters of the Dardanelles with the island called Tenedos. Homer mentioned that between Tenedos and another island called Imbros, there was a wide cavern, in which Poseidon kept his horses.

According to the Little Iliad, the Greeks were hiding on Tenedos after they pretended to leave Troy. Also there, according to the Odyssey, the Greeks leaving Troy after winning the war travelled first and made sacrifices. Between the Dardanelles and Troy stretches the plain of Scamander River, extending to the west. To the left, far on the horizon, the outline of the Mount Ida massif can be barely seen.

The viewing platform is the best place to understand how Troy VI was protected behind the massive fortifications. The circumference of these walls originally measured around 550 meters, of which 330 meters are still standing. It is the proof of the ingenuity of Trojan builders who erected the walls some 3700 years ago.

This masterwork of architecture was built of massive regular blocks of limestone and reached a height of six meters. Most probably, over the wall, there was also a mud-brick superstructure that brought the total height of the fortifications to ten meters. In the area of the Eastern Gate, two lines of walls, external and internal, can be observed, overlapping each other. At this point, there was a gate, invisible from the outside and impossible to force using a battering ram as there was no space to use it.

The walls of Troy were the spectators during the fight between the Trojan prince Hector and the Greek warrior Achilles. Hector was the son of King Priam and Queen Hecuba. During one of the battles of the Trojan War, he killed Achilles's best friend, Patroclus and thus enraged Achilles who set to avenge his fallen comrade. Hector decided to fight against Achilles in a duel, but when he saw the approaching Greek warrior, he was seized by fear and started to flee. The opponents run around the fortifications of Troy three times. If we assume that Troy VI was the Homeric city, it would mean that before the duel the heroes had run around 1.5 kilometres.

Finally, Hector mastered his fears and faced Achilles. His bravery came to nothing as goddess Athena personally supported Achilles. Even when he finally realized that his efforts were in vain, Hector decided to continue the fight and die as a hero, remembered because of his bravery in years to come. In his final words, dying Hector asked Achilles for an honourable funeral but was refused.

The walls of Troy also silently witnessed the wreath of Achilles who decided to desecrate Hector's body and let the dogs and vultures devour his flesh. It was the greatest punishment for the ancients because it meant condemning the soul to eternal wandering on earth. In addition, Achilles attached the body to his chariot and rode around the walls of Troy every morning.

Finally, even the gods could not stand watching this gruesome ritual. After twelve days, they sent two messengers: Iris and Thetis, the mother of Achilles who told him to allow King Priam to come and take the body for ransom. King Priam offered Achilles richly decorated clothes and many objects made of gold. Achilles returned the body and even offered a truce of twelve days to allow the Trojans to perform funeral rites for Hector. The last lines of the Iliad are dedicated to Hector's funeral.

While gazing upon such magnificent fortifications, it is tempting to imagine that these were the walls of the mythical Troy, besieged by the Greek army, especially that the walls seem impenetrable and the Greeks only managed to get inside using the Trojan Horse trick. Wilhelm Dörpfeld, a German archaeologist and architect, who excavated Troy at the end of the 19th century had the same idea. He argued that proper identification of Homeric Troy points to Troy VI. This idea was later undermined by an American archaeologist Carl Blegen who worked at Troy 40 years later. He claimed that small buildings and food storages from Troy VIIa indicate that this layer represents the Homeric Troy.

Temple of Athena and Troy VI bastion

Walk down from the platform and turn right to follow the marked sightseeing path along the Walls of Troy VI. First, you will pass the massive Eastern Tower from the 13th century CE, which was a later addition to the fortifications. This tower, projecting from the wall, originally had two stories, but it was only possible to get inside from the upper one.

Go past the Eastern Gate where two lines of the walls overlap. It is an opportunity to look closely at how the great blocks of limestone were fitted together. After around 50 meters you will reach the district of the Temple of Athena.

This location represents the typical situation within the Hisarlık Mound – the accumulation of multiple settlement layers and structures one on the other. Here, the sacred precinct of Athena, the goddess of wisdom, handicraft, and just warfare was erected on the bastion of the Late Bronze Age Troy. The Temple of Athena was rebuilt several times and was finally demolished, becoming the source of construction materials in the early-modern era.

You are in the location of the foundations of the Temple of Athena from the Greco-Roman times. However, the area had been used much earlier. The Northeast Bastion, the most massive

Sightseeing tour of Troy

Temple of Athena and Troy VI bastion

tower belonging to the citadel of Troy VI, once rose to a height of 9 meters. It is now ruined but still reaches 7 meters, as it was preserved as a part of the walls surrounding the Sacred District of Athena. In the later period, a narrow and steep staircase was added beside the tower, leading down to a deep well. Possibly, there was a need for fresh water during the religious rituals and festivals held in the district.

Looking around the area marked as the Temple of Athena, it is hard to believe that there once stood a magnificent building dedicated to this goddess. You can only see the foundations of the altar, fragments of marble Doric capitals, and some parts of the coffered roof, all scattered on the ground. Unfortunately, even before the excavations of Troy by Heinrich Schliemann, local people had known where to obtain excellent building materials.

The structure was the centre of the annual celebration in honour of the goddess Athena, with sacrifices and athletic contests. Its entablature, i.e. the superstructure that lies horizontally above columns, was richly decorated with reliefs, encompassing four different themes: a Gigantomachy, a Centauromachy, an Amazonomachy, and the battle between the Greeks and the Trojans, called the Ilioupersis. The best-preserved of these reliefs, depicting Apollo as Helios with four galloping horses, was found during the excavations lead by Heinrich Schliemann in 1872. It is now in the Pergamon-Museum in Berlin, Germany.

The visit to the scant ruins of the Temple of Athena offers an opportunity to take a look at the role that this goddess had played during the Trojan War. The story of the war began with the wedding of Peleus, king of Thessaly, to the sea goddess Thetis. Among the divine guests invited by Peleus, there were three goddesses: Hera, Aphrodite, and Athena. They soon became bitter rivals for a golden apple thrown among the guests by Eris, the goddess of discord, who had not been invited to the wedding. The newly-weds Peleus and Thetis later had a child, Achilles, destined to become the greatest hero of the Trojan War.

Zeus decided that Trojan prince Paris had to judge which goddess is most beautiful. In the story of the first beauty contest, where the three goddesses competed, Hera tried to bribe Paris, promising him power over all of Asia and Europe, while Athena offered him wisdom and glory in battle. Aphrodite won by promising Paris the hand of Helen. When Paris selected Aphrodite and awarded her the golden apple inscribed with the words 'for the fairest', the other two goddesses were furious. For this reason, they sided with the Greek warriors in the Trojan War.

Athena personally interfered with the events of the war many times, always supporting the Greeks. The Trojans asked for her protection in vain. Hecuba, the wife of King Priam of Troy, invited the noble women of Troy to go to the temple of Athena on the Acropolis and implore mercy by offering the goddess the most beautiful dress. However, Athena pointedly ignored their pleas for help.

The Greek colonists settled in Troy around 700 BCE, arriving probably from the islands of Tenedos and Lesbos. They must have had the tale of Athena's help for the Greeks in the Trojan

War in their minds and decided to build the sanctuary to their mythical supporter.

The exact date when they first Temple of Athena was erected as well as the details of its architecture remain unknown. It can be assumed that this Archaic Temple was of the Ionic order, as other Greek sanctuaries of that period, built-in Asia Minor and the Aegean Islands. It was probably a rather modest structure as Strabo claimed that 'It is said that the city of the present Ilians was for a time a mere village, having its temple of Athena, a small and cheap temple.'

This building was visited by Alexander the Great on his way to conquer Persia as he sacrificed to Athena and poured libations to the heroes. He also promised to construct a new temple and donated his armour to the goddess.

The popular belief states that the Hellenistic Temple was built as an initiative of Lysimachus, one of the generals of Alexander the Great. However, the latest archaeological analyses point out that its construction was initiated around 240 BCE, long after his death.

The Hellenistic Temple of Athena was partly destroyed during Gaius Flavius Fimbria's sack of Troy. The temple was later renovated at the times of Augustus who reigned from 27 BCE to 14 CE. Its plan had the dimensions of 36 to 16 meters and that a Doric colonnade surrounded the temple.

Citadel and Megaron of Troy II/III

From the area of the Temple of Athena, walk along the signposted route in the south-western direction, towards the Citadel Walls of Troy II/III. It is a very distinctive place in Troy, and you will quickly recognize it by characteristic modern roofing. After about 40 meters from the temple, you will find yourself in this pleasantly shaded area.

This site is the location of the fortifications of Troy from the period of 2550-2200 BCE, protected by the modern awning. Under the same structure, there are also the ruins of the building known as the Megaron of Troy II/III, from the same period.

Citadel and Megaron of Troy II/III

The first structure that you can see here is the fortification wall. Unlike the walls of Troy VI, erected from massive limestone blocks, these fortifications were constructed of handmade mud-bricks. They date back to the period of 2250 to 2200 BCE, known as Troy II.

The characteristic reddish colour of the bricks results from the process of their production that required firing them in a kiln. In warm regions with very little timber available to fuel a kiln, such bricks were generally sun-dried. The act of firing the bricks in Troy means that it was located in a forested area with plenty of wood readily available.

The majority of the visible stretch of the wall is a modern reconstruction that protects the original wall hidden within it, still reaching the height of four meters. If you look carefully at the lowest section of the wall, you can find an exposed fragment of the ancient wall, too.

Under the same protective roofing, next to the wall, there is a structure called the Megaron of Troy II/III. Megarons were the characteristic element of the Greek architecture of the Mycenaean period. These were long and relatively narrow halls preceded with open porches decorated with two columns. Their layout foreshadowed the later plan of Greek temples. Inside a megaron, there was a central hearth, and the smoke escaped through an opening in the roof. Megarons had many functions as they served as throne rooms, places of feasts, and religious worship. The best-known megarons can be seen in the Peloponnese in Greece, for instance at Mycenae, Tiryns, and Pylos.

The megaron you can see in Troy was excavated in the 90s of the 20th century when its mud-brick walls resting on stone foundations were revealed. The megaron was built at the same time as the adjacent fortifications. It had the characteristic central hearth and the traces on the floor indicated that it was covered with reed mats.

This megaron was not the only one discovered at Troy, but the others, to the north, have been only partly excavated. Beautifully decorated ceramics found inside the building suggest that it was used for some religious activities and this presumption is strengthened by the base below one of the walls, thought to have served as an altar. The most magnificent of the finds, the ritual vessel with two handles in the shape of humans, is now in the collections of the Trojan Museum, situated near the archaeological site of Troy. Other finds include metal, rock crystal, horn, agate, and faïence objects as well as figurines and the knob of a sceptre, possibly brought from Egypt. The megaron was destroyed by fire, dated to 2290-2200 BCE, but parts of its whitewashed walls have been preserved up to a height of 1.5 meters.

The curiously looking roof was erected in 2003 to protect the precious ancient buildings in a way that allowed the visitors to see them at the same time. The roof was designed to demonstrate the original height of the Hisarlık Mound before it was significantly reduced during the excavations carried out in the 19th century by Heinrich Schliemann.

The shape of the roof recalls a sail of a ship, billowing in the wind. This reflects the motto that the wind brought wealth to Troy. Strong north-easterly winds made many ancient sailors wait in the nearby bay before travelling to the Black Sea. They must have spent a lot of their wealth in Troy, awaiting for the moment when the almost incessant winds finally stopped.

Fortification Walls of Troy I

Follow the sightseeing path in the eastern direction. When you leave the shaded area of the Citadel Walls and the Megaron of Troy II/III, walk for around 20 meters. There you will reach the next stop, the Fortification Walls of Troy I. These walls constitute the most ancient layer of Trojan buildings, dating back to around 2920 BCE. There is a stretch of defensive walls with a tower-like projection as well as the southern gate.

The name of this stop – Troy I – means that you are now standing in the place where the oldest traces of human settlement within the Hisarlık Mound have been found. The history of the city dates back to the Early Bronze Age, i.e. around the year 3000 BCE, when the first settlement was established here. It was a small village, built on terraces of the hill, and consisting of 20 tiny rectangular houses. They were erected from interconnected blocks of stone and bricks. Despite the modest size, it was a flourishing mercantile centre, because its location allowed to control of the trade traffic through the Dardanelles – the route taken by every merchant ship from the Aegean Sea to the Black Sea. This first phase of Troy lasted for a very long time, until around 2500 BCE as testified by the accumulation of deposits, reaching four meters in depth.

Stone walls, repeatedly strengthened, protected the first settlement of Troy. These walls were erected on bedrock, which means that underneath there are no traces of human activity. In this stretch of the walls, there was a southern gate, two meters wide. The walls are tilted slightly to the inside of the settlement.

The modest settlement within the walls was a roughly circular area, with a diameter of 90 meters. At the defence tower, that forms a part of these fortifications, a fascinating stele has been found. It is adorned with a relief showing the upper half of the human body, possibly with the weapon. The tradition of erecting such stelai in Troy was a long-lasting one, as similar upright blocks were also found near the gate of Troy VI which existed one millennium later.

Sightseeing tour of Troy

Fortification Walls of Troy I

Manor House of Troy II

From the Fortification Walls of Troy I, follow the sightseeing path in the north-western direction. After around 30 meters, you will reach the site of the Manor House of Troy II. From this location, there are also panoramic views towards the Dardanelles and the vast Trojan plain. This site consists of three parallel longhouses of the megaron type, dating back to the period of 2550 BC-2300 BCE. The fortifications protected these manor houses, but there was also a lower city outside the walls.

Troy II consisted of seven layers of settlement, lying one on the other. In comparison to Troy I, Troy II was an extensive settlement, and the inhabitants of the upper city enjoyed many luxuries, such as silver, gold, and amber jewellery, found during the excavations of Schliemann. They also knew how to use a potter's wheel to produce beautifully decorated ceramics.

The prosperity of Troy II offers us a chance at looking closer at the trading links of this city, situated in the Troad, and other regions of Europe and Asia. In the modern era, where all the parts

The Secrets of Troy

Manor House of Troy II

of the world are connected, and it is possible to buy the most exotic products, it is easy to assume that in the ancient period people had to rely on locally obtained materials.

The case of Troy demonstrates that this assumption is false. The Trojans purchased amber from the coasts of the Baltic Sea, tin from the Ore Mountains, situated in Germany and the Czech Republic, and from Central Asia. Faïence was brought from Egypt and Palestine while nephrite and lapis lazuli were imported from the region of Afghanistan, and iron from Iran. The Trojans also traded with Sicily, mainland Greece and the Greek islands, Cyprus, and the sites of the Black Sea coast.

The most impressive building within the upper city of Troy II is the Megaron IIA, also dubbed the Aristocratic Residence or the Manor House. Unfortunately for the visitors, not much can be seen in this location, only the outlines of the megaron's walls. There is much more underground because the archaeologists covered the building with earth to protect it. Thus, it is necessary to use much imagination to visualize this massive structure, 30 meters long and 14 meters wide. The walls of the building ended with vertical wooden posts, and this architectural solution was recreated in the modern era, to mark the location of the building's corners. The megaron is also the place where huge rectangular blocks of stone were used for the first time – an impressive feat, particularly when we realize that the iron tools would not have been available for another millennium.

Schliemann's Trench

From the Manor House of Troy II, follow the path to the west. Just 20 meters away, you will reach the platform over the Schliemann's Trench. Directly below this platform, there are traces of a stone wall, thought to be a rampart of Troy I. The mud-brick wall to your right is a modern structure that protects the trench.

In front of you, there are several parallel stone walls erected with the herringbone technique, meaning that the stones were put in diagonally. These walls are among the oldest objects found in Troy because they are the foundations of the Early Bronze Age houses from around 2920 BCE.

Schliemann's Trench is a reminder of the actions of the famous Heinrich Schliemann, frequently dubbed the discoverer of Troy. In search of the castle of King Priam described by Homer in the Iliad, Schliemann made a huge trench in Hisarlık mound, 40 meters wide and 17 meters deep, oriented along the north-south axis. It was dug through the centre of the mound between 1871 and 1873 as the test-trench reaching bedrock.

The person most commonly associated with the discovery of Troy in the modern era is, most certainly, Heinrich Schliemann, a German amateur archaeologist, and adventurer. He was also great at self-promotion and built a web of legends and tales about himself, including the story of how at the age of seven, he had already claimed that one day he would excavate the ancient Troy.

However, his ambitions had to be put on a shelf for many years, as he gathered the necessary funds, starting as an apprentice at a grocery and a cabin boy on the steamer bound for Venezuela. Many years later, after many successful business decisions, when he was 46, Schliemann accumulated a vast fortune and was able to start the search for Troy. He was only able to find it because of the

Schliemann's Trench

suggestions of Frank Calvert whose family owned the area of the Hisarlık Mound.

Schliemann's Trench is a perfect example of how desperate Schliemann was to discover the Homeric Troy. As he was confident that this legendary city must be in the lowest layer of the settlement, the workers dug hastily through all the higher layers, to quickly reach the target. This method stands in stark contrast with the techniques of modern archaeology when all the layers are carefully studied. However, Schliemann was not educated as an archaeologist, and he had only one dream: to find the city of King Priam.

Today, scholars agree that Schliemann's excavations destroyed the layer of the 'real Troy', the city that could be dated to be contemporary with the legendary Trojan War. Ironically, Schliemann's actions completed the task of the Greeks trying to destroy Troy as he razed the walls of this city to the ground. His search for Troy also resulted in irreversible damage to the site and the loss of much valuable information.

Despite the significant loss of knowledge caused by digging the trench, this place enables a better understanding of the multiple

Sightseeing tour of Troy

layers of Troy, similar to the layers of a gigantic wedding cake, visible when the first slice is cut out. Standing with your back to the foundations of the Early Bronze Age houses, you can see the levels of Troy, carefully marked by archaeologists.

The lowest layer visible here is Troy II and to see the level of Troy IX you need to look up. The span between these layers represents a period of more than two and a half millennia. This profile is the result of the work of Schliemann's assistant Wilhelm Dörpfeld who continued his work, and much later excavations of Manfred Korfmann.

Walls, Gate, and Ramp of Troy II

From Schliemann's Trench, walk along the sightseeing route in the south-western direction. After some 35 meters you will get to the location of the Ramp of Troy II. From this place, you can see the Walls of Troy II and the Ramp – its appearance is the result of partial reconstruction.

The wooden viewing platform on which you are standing offers a great close-up view of the ramp, but you can also climb up the second platform, to get a broader perspective of the fortifications. The paved ramp led through a massive gate into the interior of Troy II. The city was protected by high walls, built of mud bricks on the limestone substructure. These walls, around 330 meters long, surrounded the area of about 9000 square meters. The visible construction dates back to around 2300 BCE.

In the tale of the Trojan War, the main gate to the city, through which the Trojans went out to fight the Greek warriors on the plain below, was called the Scaean Gate. When the Trojan prince Hector was dying, his last words were directed to his killer, Achilles. He prophesied Achilles's death that would soon follow: 'I know you what you are, and was sure that I should not move you, for your heart is hard as iron; look to it that I bring not heaven's anger upon you on the day when Paris and Phoebus Apollo, valiant though you be, shall slay you at the Scaean gates.'

This prophecy was quickly fulfilled, Achilles died while scaling the gate of Troy, hit with an arrow shot by Prince Paris, the brother

The Secrets of Troy

Ramp of Troy II

of Hector, but guided by Apollo himself. The arrow hit the hero's heel, the only vulnerable part of his body because, when his mother Thetis dipped him in the River Styx as an infant, she held him by one of his heels.

Many centuries passed after the events described by Homer. When Schliemann excavated at this location, he was convinced that this was the gate that Homer had featured. His belief resulted from three pieces of the puzzle. First of all, the splendid ramp could easily be imagined as the walkway for the Trojan warriors. Secondly, Troy II was destroyed by a great fire as testified by the layer of ashen remains, two meters thick. Again, this fact perfectly fits with the legendary destruction of the Homeric Troy after the Greeks got inside using the Trojan Horse. Finally, near the ramp, Schliemann made one of the most amazing discoveries in the history of Troy's excavations.

In 1873, near the ramp, Schliemann made one of his most sensational discoveries. He found a rich collection of objects, consisting of copper pots, terra cotta goblets, bronze and copper weapons, such as shields, knives, lance heads, and daggers. There were also

Sightseeing tour of Troy

six silver knife blades, mistakenly identified by Schliemann as coins. However, these listed objects were not the most fantastic part of the collection. The treasure also consisted of silver and gold objects, for instance, a silver vase that contained two extraordinary gold diadems, dubbed by Schliemann as the jewels of Helen. There were also thousands of gold rings and buttons, two gold cups, and six gold bracelets. The collection was completed with other silver vases and a cup made of electrum – a mixture of gold, silver, and copper.

Enthusiastic Schliemann was sure that he had found the treasure of King Priam, and magnificent gold necklaces and earrings once had belonged to the beautiful mythical Helen. In fact, as demonstrated by the dating of the layers of Troy settlements, carried out later, these items had been much older. They were assigned to Troy II which had existed 1,200 years before the destruction of the Homeric Troy.

Schliemann was married to his own beautiful Helen when he excavated at Troy. However, he met her in far less dramatic and romantic circumstances. When Schliemann decided to search for Troy, he realized that he would need a personal assistant with the knowledge of Greek history and culture. He even put an advert that he was looking for a wife in an Athenian newspaper. His bride was a relative of the Archbishop of Athens. Her name was Sophia Engastromenos, and when 47-year-old Schliemann married her, she was only 17. Her best-known photo shows her wearing the ancient treasures discovered Schliemann at Troy. The marriage had three children with highly symbolic names: Andromache, Troy, and Agamemnon.

Enchanted by the treasure, Schliemann secretly took away the rich collection from Asia Minor.When the Ottoman authorities learned about this fact, Schliemann's permission to conduct the excavations in Troy was revoked, and the Ottoman official who was the supervisor of the works in Troy was imprisoned. Amazingly, Schliemann later recovered the permission in exchange for the return of the part of the treasure.

Palatial Residence of Troy VI

Palatial Residence of Troy VI

From the Ramp of Troy II follow the path to the south. On the way, there is a viewing point where the Dardanelles Strait is clearly visible in the background, with the Trojan Plain between you and its waters. According to the archaeologists, the harbour of Late Bronze Age Troy was situated over there, around 8 kilometres from the fortifications of the city. The researchers believe that the landscape of that era matched the descriptions provided by Homer.

After 20 meters you will get to the stop where the traces of the Palatial Residence of Troy VI can be seen. Not much has been preserved from this structure, but it probably had two floors as a fragment of a staircase was discovered. Schliemann called this building 'the Palace of Priam', but the residence dates back to the earlier period of 1700-1300 BCE. Large vessels for storing food discovered here testify to the fact that, at least for some time, this building served as a warehouse.

The observation point of the Palatial Residence has been con-

Sightseeing tour of Troy

structed directly above the massive fortifications of Troy VI. From this vantage point, the retaining wall of the complex can be seen to your left. It was an impressive construction, 27 meters long, gently sloping inwards. Four vertical offsets, sometimes described as the 'saw teeth', are the most characteristic feature of the wall. Their creation required high precision in cutting the massive blocks. These offsets played, most possibly, two roles: as the decoration and as a support for the timber-frame superstructure that was filled with mud-bricks. The slight curvature of the wall, on the other hand, could have been a measure against the earthquakes. While looking at these walls, it is easy to understand why Homer repeatedly praised the beautiful walls of Ilios.

The building that this substructure supported was located on the lowest of the terraces that formed the mound of Troy. A broad alley separated the residence from the fortifications. Based on the impressive dimensions of the building, the researchers assume that it was a part of a larger palatial complex. Troy VI was a carefully planned city with a unified architectural design and the streets of equal width, running up to the heart of the town. However, the identity of the palatial complex is sometimes questioned, and the functions of its rooms have not been discovered. As large vessels – the pithoi – were found within the building, it could also be a warehouse for the foodstuffs.

Western Sanctuary of Troy

Leave the viewpoint next to the Palatial Residence of Troy VI and follow the sightseeing route to the south. After 20 meters, you will reach the point overlooking the Western Sanctuary. It is situated in the south-western part of the city while the Athena Sanctuary is on the opposite side of the mound, on the north-eastern side. The Western Sanctuary developed directly outside the walls of the Late Bronze Age citadel, on the site overlooking the Dardanelles.

The temple complex was built during the Archaic period of ancient Greece, but the sanctuary was also used later, during the Hellenistic and Roman times, with some modifications. The visible remains of buildings of the Sanctuary date back to the period

Western Sanctuary

of Troy VIII and IX. They were erected on the ruins of earlier buildings of Troy VI and VII, perhaps also serving some religious purposes. The best-preserved structure is an altar of the so-called Lower Sanctuary. There are also several wells, which were used for the collection of the blood of sacrificial animals and drawing water.

The first impression of the space within the Western Sanctuary is of a chaotic architecture of this sacred place. It results from frequent modifications and additions made over the centuries to the religious precinct, probably first constructed around 700 BCE. As time passed, the space became adorned with increasingly impressive buildings. There were three main altars, now called A, B, and C, used at the same time. It means that most probably there were several different deities worshipped within the sanctuary. Unfortunately, the names of these deities have not been discovered. However, there are some essential archaeological clues as to their identity, for instance, numerous terracotta statuettes of Demeter and Kybele.

Another significant clue that may indicate the identity of the goddess worshipped in the Western Sanctuary is provided by over

Sightseeing tour of Troy

400 fragments of vessels decorated with painted birds, mainly swans. Swans are highly symbolic birds in many cultures because of their particular behaviour. They are migratory and thus are related to the changing seasons. Their eggs are frequently interpreted as symbols of fertility.

Moreover, swans are known to find a mate for life, and so they are also associated with love and marriage. Finally, just before they die, they produce a peculiar sound, known as the swan song. This fact became proverbial in ancient Greece, as the description of a final gesture, effort, or performance given just before death.

There is also a connection between the swans and the legend of the Trojan War. The link is provided by the history of the Spartan Queen Leda, the wife of Tyndareus. The king of gods, Zeus, admired and seduced her, in the guise of a swan escaping from an eagle. The same night Leda also lay with her husband, and later laid two eggs from which Helen, Clytemnestra, Castor, and Pollux were hatched.

While it is uncertain which of the children were mortal and which – divine, it was always sure that Helen was the daughter of Zeus. Later, Helen would become the wife of King Menelaus of Sparta, from whom she was abducted by Prince Paris, in the sequence of events leading to the Trojan War. This story is the most probable explanation as to why the Trojans would use swan-decorated vessels in their religious rituals.

The exact identity of the deities worshipped in the Western Sanctuary is unknown, but the scholars are confident that at least some of them were female. Apart from the statuettes of Demeter and Kybele, also the swan-decorated vessels indicate the possible names of these goddesses. Swans are shown pulling the chariot of Aphrodite, and she is riding on them. This goddess of beauty was the winner of the Apple for the Fairest contest that initiated the series of incidents resulting in the Trojan War. Moreover, Artemis is also associated with wild animals, as is Kybele. It is even possible that all of them were worshipped at Troy, through rituals of sacrifice, consumption of small quantities of food and drink in

The Secrets of Troy

specially produced ritual vessels, and with performances involving the skins of wild animals.

Lower City of Troy

Walk along the Western Sanctuary, following the path further to the south, and then turn to the right. After 25 meters you will get to the Lower City of Troy, situated outside the Upper City of Troy on the Hisarlık Mound, and stretching far beyond its fortifications. This outer settlement was also protected by a defensive system consisting of a 4-meter-wide ditch paired with a palisade, enclosing an area measuring between 25 and 35 ha.

The Lower City of Troy VI/VIIa (13th-14th century BCE) stretches outside the citadel, to the west. Stone foundations of numerous houses have been identified here. The most spectacular finds from the Lower City include a bronze statuette and a terracotta bull figurine. Excavations are still being conducted in this area, bringing new, exciting discoveries every year.

The main sightseeing path of ancient Troy focuses on the traces of this ancient city within the fortification walls. The vast Lower City has not been thoroughly examined, as less than two percent of this residential area has been excavated so far. Much information about it has been gained through magnetic prospection.

As most of the people lived here, outside the central citadel, it means that there is still much to learn about their lives, customs, and practices. One of the excavated buildings – the Terrace House of Troy VI – had several rooms with a second story, and it may have served religious purposes as evidenced by the finds: a bronze statuette and the ceramic image of a bull. One thing is sure: the comfortable lives of the Lower City inhabitants finished abruptly when Troy VIIa was destroyed, as confirmed by the finds from the destruction level: weapons, skeletons, and burnt remains. The relationship of these objects with the events described in the Iliad is a subject of much scholarly debate.

After the destruction of Troy VIIa, the immigrants settled within the citadel, but only a few buildings were constructed outside the walls. These newly arrived people were most probably from the

Sightseeing tour of Troy

Lower City

Balkans or the Lower Danube region. They brought with them the tradition of handmade pottery. Their living conditions within the small area of the citadel were very crowded, the earlier squares and streets had to be built over with houses, filled with large storage vessels – the pithoi.

By this time, Troy had lost much of its geographically strategic importance because it was no longer near the coast, due to the silting of the Simois and Scamander rivers. Moreover, other cities such as Sigeion, Achilleion, and Abydos were founded nearby, replacing Troy in geopolitical importance.

The existence of the Lower City was an indicator of Troy's periods of prosperity: while this area was virtually abandoned in the late II millennium BCE, it was revived by the arrival of the Greek colonists around 750 BCE.

It expanded even more when the city became part of the Roman Empire. In these times, there was considerable activity in the large residential district of the Lower City. This external settlement stretched in the dense configuration of buildings to the west, east, and south of the central citadel. Many of the dwellings were richly decorated villas, with mosaic floors and painted ceilings. The streets of the Lower City were wide and paved with stones, reaching 5 meters in width.

In time, Troy declined again, after a series of devastating earthquakes that shook the city around 500 CE. They destroyed the functioning waterways by turning them into swamps. These disastrous events were soon followed by the outbreak of malaria and the bubonic plague. As in the Late Bronze Age, the remaining Trojans once again took shelter on within the citadel and abandoned the Lower City. The last traces of the city's existence are several late-sixth-century coins. Thus, when the Ottoman Sultan Mehmed II arrived at the ruined citadel in 1462, the site had been abandoned for around a millennium. Mehmed II regarded the Trojan warriors as his kinsmen as his speech made during the visit emphasized his conquest of Constantinople as the vengeance for the Trojans' defeat by the Greeks. This act clearly shows the power of memories surrounding Troy that are still repeated and recalled in the modern culture and show business.

Water Cave of Wilusa

Water Cave of Wilusa is a place located off the main sightseeing path of Troy. From the Lower City of Troy take a narrow path through the meadows and fields, pleasantly shaded by many trees. After walking for around 150 meters in the south-western direction, you will reach the Water Cave of Wilusa.

Water Cave of Wilusa is an artificial cave, not a work of nature. A 160-meter-long corridor was cut in the rock, heading eastward. It is connected to the surface by four vertical shafts with a height of up to 17 meters. The corridor was made in the third millennium BCE. It means that in the heyday of Troy VI, the cave had already been in use for a thousand years.

The cave is a relatively new archaeological discovery, as it was found and researched in the years 1997-2001. The prehistoric cave served as the water distribution system, from which water flowed to several rock-cut basins. The Roman engineers added clay pipes

Sightseeing tour of Troy

Water Cave of Wilusa

that directed the flow into ponds outside the cave.

During the times of peace, the Trojans had no problems regarding the water supply as the location of their city guaranteed freshwater from numerous rivers and streams. The most important of these rivers were Scamander and Simois, both having their sources in Mount Ida. According to Homer, the gods of these rivers, of the same names, supported the Trojans during the war with the Greeks.

However, during the sieges, the city needed to collect and store the water, and for this reason, wells and cisterns were built within the citadel. In the south-eastern part of the Lower City, the most astonishing solution for the water supply was created, now known as the Water Cave of Wilusa. This artificial cave with long underground tunnels collected rainwater and the water from an underground source. Later, the Romans solved the water-supply issues by building a system consisting of clay pipes, such as displayed in the Pithos Garden, and an impressive aqueduct, still standing in Kemerdere, some 12 kilometres to the south-east of Troy.

Why are the artificial tunnels below the Lower City now known as the Water Cave of Wilusa and not of Troy? According to some scholars Troy can be identified with the Late Bronze Age city of Wilusa, mentioned several times in the 13th century BCE in Hittite sources as a part of the Assuwa confederation.

This identification is based on several factors. First of all, the alternate names for Troy in ancient Greek language were Ilios and Ilion, and these are linked etymologically to Wilusa. Even more importantly, the archaeological excavations in the region of the Troad have demonstrated that in the 13th century BCE, Troy had no major rival and was most probably the capital of a city-state and a regional superpower.

The biggest problem of the link between Troy and Wilusa results from the lack of any locally written sources that could confirm it. All the documents discussing Wilusa were written by the Hittites who exchanged correspondence with the rulers of Wilusa. Possibly there is still an archive to be discovered within the ruins of Troy that would clarify all the uncertainties.

One of such Hittite documents concerning Wilusa is the Alaksandu of Wilusa Treaty, dating to around 1280 BCE, signed between Alaksandu and the Hittite king, Muwatalli II. This document discusses the allegiance of the vassal monarch, Alaksandu, to the Hittite Empire. The fascinating element of the treaty is the list of divinities that guarantee good auspices and provide the guarantee that the agreement would be respected.

One of them is Apaliunas, sometimes likened to the Greek god Apollo. The other one, vouching on behalf of Troy, is much more mysterious. It is called Kaskalkur, a local goddess of springs who would reside in the Water Cave of Wilusa. Finally, it is worth mentioning that the name of Alaksandu is sometimes interpreted as a distortion of the Greek name Alexandros. It would provide the link to the legend of the Trojan War as Paris of Troy was also known as Alexandros of Ilios.

The cult of Apollo was a crucial element of the religious beliefs of the Trojans, as attested by Homer. The best illustration of this fact is the story of beautiful virgin Chryseis. Her father was a Trojan priest of Apollo at Chryse, near the city of Troy. She was taken as prisoner by Achilles but was later given to Agamemnon who claimed his right to her as the king. Agamemnon was so enchanted with Chryseis that refused to allow her father to ransom her with the gifts of gold and silver. Desperate Chryses begged Apollo to bring revenge on the Greeks, and the god listened to this request, sending the plague onto the Greek army. Thus, Chryseis was returned to her father. Agamemnon compensated himself for this loss by taking another captive, Briseis, from Achilles. This situation became a source of conflict between Agamemnon and Achilles, the main theme of the Iliad.

The most enigmatic word in the prayer of Chryses to Apollo is 'Sminthe'. The ancient Greeks had already found this word incomprehensible and attributed its origins to one of the Anatolian languages. Unfortunately, the epic poem of Homer does not provide any hints at the meaning of this word, but it is often explained on the basis of the context in which it had been used in The Iliad. Since Apollo had sent the plague on the Greeks, he was associated with rodents as major disease carriers. Therefore, Apollo, as the god that could send an epidemic, was given the title of the 'Lord of Mice'. Moreover, some 50 km to the south of Troy, the archaeologists discovered a temple identified with the one dedicated to Apollo Smintheus. This location, in the village of Gülpınar, is associated with the ancient Chrysa where Chryses was the priest of Apollo's cult.

Odeon of Troy

Walk from the Water Cave of Wilusa following the same path back to the Lower City of Troy. In this location, get back on the main sightseeing trail, and follow it to the east. After around 130 meters, you will get to the odeon of Troy. Beyond this small theatre, you can see the walls of Troy VI and the single column of the Pillar-House from the same time.

If you turn around, on the other side of the path, you can glimpse the scant remains of the Roman-period baths. The bouleuterion, i.e. the council chamber of the city, is situated some 60 meters to the east. The bouleuterion was a place of political gath-

Odeion

erings and this building in Troy, originating from the time of Augustus, still has a podium and the first row of marble seats. All these buildings are located on the fringes of the central square of the city's public life called the agora.

The odeon of Troy, originating most probably from the time of Emperor Octavian Augustus, still has a podium and several rows of marble seats. This building served as a concert-hall as its Greek name means the place for the recitation of odes. Decorative marble blocks, lying in front of the odeon, were once a part of its scaenae frons, i.e. the stage building. It was first discovered by Wilhelm Dörpfeld in 1893 but did not receive much attention from archaeologists until recently.

The Greeks and Romans who lived in Troy during the so-called phases VIII and IX were very clearly conscious about the mythical past of their city. They even called it Ilion or Ilium to emphasize the connection with the Homeric city. Whether or not they believed in the story told in the Iliad is unclear, but they undoubtedly exploited the myth for political and economic advantages.

Sightseeing tour of Troy

The walled citadel of Troy remained the core of the city, but it played a role in the up-keeping of the mythical aura. The town attracted many prominent visitors and was the centre of tourism as much as its ruins are today. There is even good literary evidence that the city had a treasury of Trojan War relics with some of the artefacts of Bronze Age date, discovered during the construction of the Greek city.

One of the best-known visitors to Troy was Alexander the Great. He was enchanted by the ancient stories as told by Homer in the Iliad and the Odyssey. His stay at Troy was marked with many highly symbolic gestures. Not only did he sacrifice to Athena, but he also poured libations to the heroes of the Greek army. Then, he smeared himself with oil and ran a raced naked with his companions around the site. He crowned with a wreath the column which marks the grave of Achilles, remarking that Achilles had been happy in having found a faithful friend while he lived and a great poet to sing of his deeds after his death.

During the Roman times, the importance of Troy was further strengthened by its recognition as the mother city of the Romans. They believe that they were the descendants of the Trojan hero, Aeneas, who fled the city after its fall, and after many adventures settled in Latium. He was known as the ancestor of Romulus and Remus, the founder of Rome.

Aeneas was the hero of the Trojan War, born to the prince of Darnadania called Anchises and the goddess Aphrodite. Priam, the king of Troy, was his uncle and Aeneas became the leader of the Trojans' Dardanian allies. Aeneas' mother Aphrodite frequently came to his aid on the battlefield; he was also a favourite of Apollo. Even Poseidon, who usually favoured the Greeks, hurried to Aeneas's rescue after he fell under the assault of Achilles. Such mighty support from the gods signalled as-yet-unknown destiny of the honourable warrior.

Aeneas was one of the few Trojans who were not killed or enslaved when their city fell. Instead, he was commanded by the gods to flee and gathered a group of his closest associates and family, including his father Anchises and his son Ascanius. The group travelled for a long time, visiting Thrace, Delos, Crete, and Carthage on their way, to finally reach Italy. Latinus, king of the Latins, welcomed Aeneas's group and let them stay in his domain. He even offered him his daughter, Lavinia, as the wife.

Emperor Hadrian was one of the most prominent tourists who visited Troy in Roman times. He arrived in 124 CE, searching for the reminders of the myths and legends. During his stay, this emperor, known to be enamoured with Greek culture, restored the Tomb of Ajax and composed an epigram for the Tomb of Hector. He even possibly presented this poem in the city's odeon.

Hadrian's visits to the tombs of the Greek and Trojan heroes were to demonstrate that he honoured both sides of the Trojan War as their territories were then parts of the Roman Empire. Hadrian also initiated the renovation of the odeon, adding the decorative stage building. The most important material evidence of the emperor's visit is his larger-than-life cuirassed statue, discovered in the odeon in 1993. It is now on display in the Trojan Museum, accompanied by the sculpted head of Augustus, also found in the odeon.

The odeon is the last point of the Troy Tour so afterwards follow the sightseeing path in the easterly direction. It will take you to the exit – after walking for 110 meters, you will get back to the square with the Eternal Stone of Troy. From this point you walk next to the Pithos Garden and the replica of the Trojan Horse, reaching the exit after 100 meters.

Visitor tips for Troy

Troy is a historical site inscribed onto UNESCO's World Heritage List since 1998. Visiting the ruins of Troy is possible every day during the opening hours: in the summer season (April to October) from 8:30 am to 7:30 pm, and in the winter season (November to March) from 8:30 am to 5:30 pm. Please note that the ticket office closes half an hour earlier.

The ticket to Troy costs 42 TL. Children below 8 enter for free. There is also a possibility to purchase a combined ticket to Troy

Sightseeing tour of Troy

and the nearby Troy Museum for 60 TL.

There is only one entrance to the archaeological site of Troy. The car park next to the entrance is free of charge. Unfortunately, it is almost entirely unprotected from the sun. Take advantage of the few shady spots under some trees in the corner of the parking lot.

Troy can be visited individually, and you are assisted with the information boards, in English, German, and Turkish. You can also hire a licensed guide for the tour. Many travel agencies in Çanakkale and Eceabat organise such guided tours of Troy.

The archaeological site of Troy is situated near the small village of Tevfikiye. Most of the tourists visit Troy for just a few hours, and then return to Çanakkale or continue the journey further to the south. If you intend to stay near the archaeological site, you can find several restaurants and accommodation options in Tevfikiye village, just half a kilometre to the east of Troy.

The closest city is Çanakkale, located around 30 kilometres to the north. Regular minibuses connect Troy with Çanakkale. Their terminal, called Minibüs Garajı, is situated next to Atatürk Street, near Sarıçay Bridge. The minibuses depart roughly every hour, starting from 7 am and finishing at 7 pm. The ride takes 40 minutes and costs around 9 TL per person.

It is also possible to organise a taxi tour from Çanakkale to Troy and back, and the price depends on the result of negotiations with a driver. If you travel by car, take D550 route from Çanakkale, and turn to the west after 26 km. The turn-off is clearly signposted, and the total distance from Çanakkale is 30 km.

The Secrets of Troy

Troy Museum

With the opening of the new Trojan Museum, the visitors to Troy now have a possibility to gain much more information about this archaeological site and put its history into a much broader perspective. Most of the artefacts displayed in the museum had been previously exhibited in the Archaeological Museum in the centre of Çanakkale, far away from the site of Troy. The new arrangement makes it much easier to see these objects, and the visit to the museum is an excellent introduction to the tour of Troy.

Museum History and Organisation

In 2012, plans were announced to open a new museum facility – the Troy Museum, which was to operate next to the ruins of Troy. The Ministry of Culture and Tourism of Turkey expropriated 10 hectares for this purpose. The selection of the project of the building was an important event, and many Turkish and foreign companies took part in the competition. In 2013, the results of the competition were announced, and the winning project was selected from among more than 150 projects by an expert jury.

The winning team from Yalin Architectural Design, consisting of Ömer Selçuk Baz, Okan Bal, Cenk Kurtel, Mehmet Yılmaz and Berrin Yavuz started to work on the project. The construction of the Troy Museum was initiated in 2013, but the project experienced some difficulties and the work was halted in 2015. It resumed in 2017 and was finally completed in October of 2018. This fortunate timing allowed the first visitors to see the venue during the Year of Troy, celebrated in 2018. The total cost of the building came to 45 million TL, i.e. approximately $8 million.

Troy Museum

The team's official explanation and interpretation of the Troy Museum building is based on the idea of an 'excavated artefact'. This way of thinking led them to the creation of a robust cubic form with the sides 32 meters long. The building's height is equivalent to the pre-excavation height of ancient Troy.

The external walls of the building are wrapped in weathering steel called Corten that rusts in time. The premise is to evoke the connection between the past and the present. The design conceals all supportive functions underground while the exhibition space of 2000 square meters is located within the cube where it is divided into four floors and a terrace.

The interior of the museum is designed in the industrial style, with bare concrete walls clearly visible. The interiors are minimally furnished, and the building's concrete frame has been left exposed to retain focus on the exhibits. The transparent roof lets the sunlight into the museum. Concrete access ramps connect all the floors of the museum, wrapping around the inside of the cube, and making it accessible for the guests with disabilities.

Troy Museum

Troy Museum interior

The building of the Troy Museum stands out in the barren landscape of the Trojan plain, attracting the visitors' attention from afar. Whether the effect it makes on the visitors is the one that its designers aimed at, remains an open question, to be answered by the guests themselves.

The entrance to the Troy Museum entrance is accessed by a wide ramp lined with concrete walls with niches holing small exhibits. The ramp leads the visitors to the subterranean floor, with an entrance hall. This level also houses exhibition spaces, a cafe, a restaurant, and a museum shop. There are also conservation laboratories and storage space for the museum's collection, inaccessible to the visitors.

The exhibition is divided into four levels, starting at the lowest one: Cities of Troad, Layers of Troy, Ancient World, and Troy Excavation History. Above them, there is a terrace offering the views of the site of Troy and the whole region of the Troad. These four levels provide an overview of Troy and the Troad, divided into seven sections: Troad Region Archaeology, Bronze Age of

The Secrets of Troy

Entry ramp to Troy Museum

Troy, Iliad and the Trojan War, Troad and Ilion in Ancient History, Eastern Rome and Ottoman Period, History of Archaeology, and Traces of Troy.

The exhibition presents these stories along a chronological timeline highlighting technological changes, social organization, political and economic relations, urban development, daily life, arts, and craftsmanship. The visitors can explore, read, watch, contemplate, and interact with the exhibition at their own pace. Moreover, a special storyline has been prepared within the exhibition for the younger visitors, to evoke their curiosity and facilitate engagement with the artefacts.

The collections of the museum include the exhibits previously displayed in Çanakkale Archaeological Museum but also other artefacts, transferred from Istanbul Archaeological Museums and Museum of Anatolian Civilizations in Ankara. Additionally, there are 24 pieces of gold jewellery returned by the US Penn Museum in 2012. In total, the museum displays around 2,000 artefacts and has more than 40,000 artefacts in its storehouse.

Troy Museum

Troy Museum interior

Level Z – Cities of Troad

The tour of the museum starts at the lowest level where the geography of the Troad is explained. This floor offers information about ancient cities of the Troad region, including Assos, Bozcaada (Tenedos), Parion, Alexandria Troas, Apollo Smintheion, Lampsakos, Thymbria, Tavolia, and Gökçeada (Imbros).

The central space of the floor is the exhibition area devoted to these sites, while the corridor around this space offers access to a cloakroom, a cafeteria, a shop, toilets, and a conference hall. The exhibitions displayed in the corridor include a collection of the amphorae, column capitals, and tombstones. Moreover, this is also the space for temporary exhibitions.

The Secrets of Troy

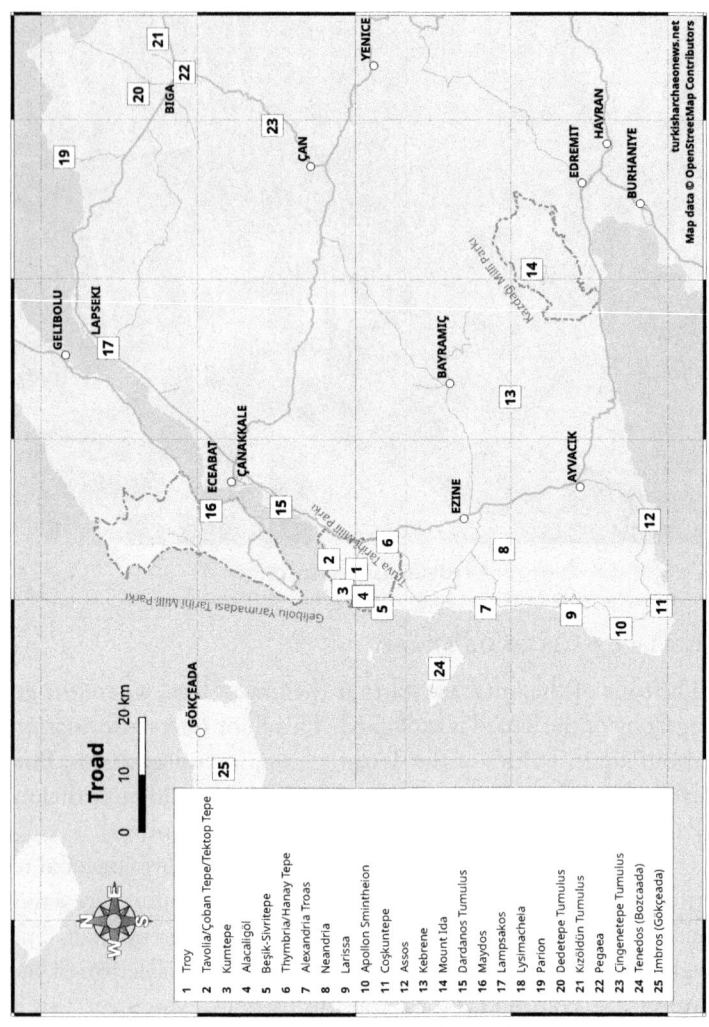

Archaeological sites of Troad

Aegean Islands

Many finds exhibited in the museum come from two Turkish islands in the Aegean Sea. Tenedos (Bozcaada) is an Aegean island, already mentioned in the Iliad. The biggest attraction from the

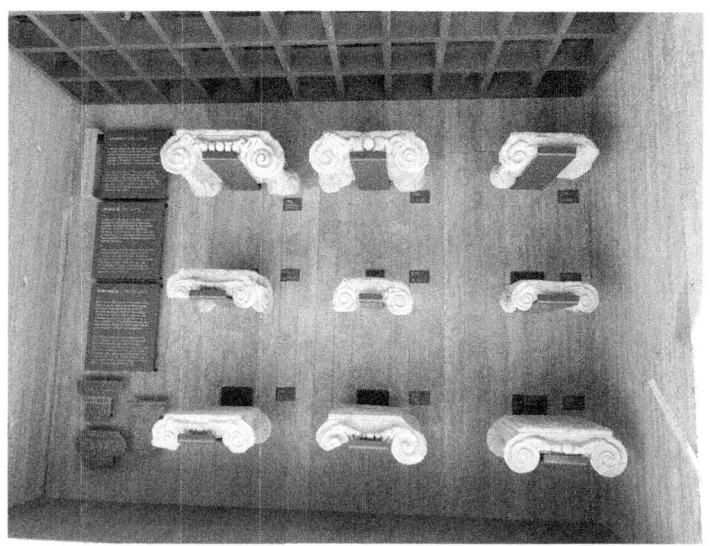

Column capitals on Level Z

island of Bozcaada (ancient Tenedos) are the exhibits found in the local necropolis during rescue excavations. This cemetery was in use for an incredibly long period: from around 3000 BCE to the 19th century CE. These finds include the vessels from the 9th century BCE, local wine and olive oil jars (so-called askoi) made from grey clay, dated to the 7th century BCE, Corinthian pottery, also from the 7th century BCE, red-figure pottery from the 5th and 4th centuries BCE, and figurines of the goddess Cybele from the 5th century BCE.

Moreover, the artefacts from the necropolis encompass stone masonry tombs, sarcophagi, pithoi, and urns. The burial gifts from the Archaic to the Hellenistic period shed light on the cultural interactions between the inhabitants of Tenedos and other regions, including continental Greece and Asia Minor.

The most valuable finds from the second Aegean island – Imbros (Gökçeada) – have been found in the area of Yenibademli Höyük archaeological site. Archaeological research has been conducted there since 1996, and seven architectural layers have been

Finds from Tenedos

identified so far. The oldest of them contains examples of so-called Cyclopean walls and Mycenaean ceramics. The depth of each cultural layer varies from 3 to 5 meters.

The inhabitants of this fortified settlement consumed lamb, goat, beef, and pork as well as marine products. This is a diet similar to their counterparts on the mainland, including Troy. Also, the houses, pottery, and tools do not show any differences from the ones found at Troy. A statue of a seated woman from the 2nd century BCE and some vessels have been brought to Troy Museum.

Dardanos Tumulus

Fascinating finds have been collected from Dardanos Tumulus. Its discovery occurred by accident, during construction works for a nearby cement factory, conducted in 1959. When the burial chamber was found, archaeological research was undertaken by a team composed of employees of museums from Istanbul and Çanakkale, under the leadership of Rüstem Duyuran. After a long break, the next series of excavations were conducted from 1989. The motivation for the second round of research was a detected attempt of robbery of the tomb.

Judging from the fragments of pottery the settlement of Dardanos was founded in the 7th or the 6th century BCE, in the time of Greek colonization of Troad from the island of Lesbos. It is also known that in times of domination of Athens, Dardanos paid a tribute of one talent to the Delian League.

The inscriptions on the walls of the tomb indicate that it was built in the late 6th century BCE by a wealthy citizen of Dardanos called Skamandrios or on his behalf. The tumulus was the burial place for an extended period, until the 1st or the 2nd century CE. When it ceased to be used for this purpose, the entrance to the hall was closed by boulders, and its exterior was masked by mud and debris.

The essential contents of the tomb were funeral gifts. Around 470 items have been discovered there, including terracotta figurines, oil lamps, perfume bottles, pieces of woollen clothes, baskets, wooden musical instruments, and pieces of furniture. Metal products make an impressive set of 85 items; that consists of jewellery and tools made of gold, silver, bronze, iron, and lead.

The most spectacular discovery of Dardanos Tumulus was a collection of gold jewellery, including crowns, wreaths, medallions, earrings, necklaces, and rings, mainly from the Hellenistic period. The finds discovered during these excavations can be found in the museum. The visitors are greatly impressed by golden diadems and wreaths, dated to the 4th and the 3rd centuries BCE, and the treasures from the necropolis (dated to the 4th century BCE), including gold jewellery, statues, and pottery.

In addition, the excavations in the area of the tumulus and its surroundings have resulted in the discovery of Hellenistic terracotta figurines, a collection of statues of Aphrodite and Eros, and ceramics from the period between the 4th and the 2nd century CE. Among these, the most striking piece is the 1st century BCE terracotta copy of the 4th-century statue of Cnidian Aphrodite by

Finds from Dardanos

the famous sculptor Praxiteles. The goddess is depicted wearing jewellery in the shape of snakes.

Tavolia and Thymbria

Tavolia and Thymbria are two less-known sites of the Troad represented in the museum. Tavolia, also called Çoban Tepe or Tektop Tepe, is the prehistoric settlement is located on the southern shore of the Dardanelles, 2 kilometres to the north-east of Kumkale. The settlement spread to the south-west from a sheer cliff overlooking the Dardanelles. No excavations have been made at this location so far, but the surface finds date back to the Early Bronze Age (corresponding to Troy I) and the Late Bronze Age (Troy VI). The site was discovered during the Troy excavations of the Cincinnati University in 1932. It was assumed that Çoban Tepe is the same site as Tavolia named by J. Calvert.

The site identified with Thymbria, situated 6.5 km to the southeast of Troy, is now called Hanay Tepe. The prehistoric finds were discovered on the southern slope of the settlement while Frank

Calvert first excavated it in 1853. His work was groundbreaking as at the time it was the first systematic excavation of a stratified site. Financial support provided by Heinrich Schliemann permitted allowed Calvert to continue excavations in 1878-79. The earliest layer of the site dates back to Troy I and the latest one – to the Byzantine times. The most important finds from Thymbria are wheel-made ceramics from the 2nd millennium BCE.

Assos

One of the most impressive collections in the museum is the one from Assos (now known as Behramkale). In the Iliad, there is information that a certain Elastos, killed by Agamemnon, had come from Pedasos, located on a steep mountain, near Satnoieis River. From this geographical description, it can be concluded that Pedasos was the same city that later was known as Assos.

However, the ancient geographer Strabo, who lived at the turn of the first century BCE and the first century CE, wrote that Pedasos, one of Lelege cities, was abandoned in his times. This statement belies the theory that Pedasos can be equated with Assos, which was inhabited continuously from the moment of its founding in the 7th century BCE.

Archaeological findings help to reconstruct the history of Assos from the days when it was founded in the 7th century BCE by Aeolian settlers. Most probably, they settled in the area that had been previously inhabited from the prehistoric times. The Greeks came to Asia Minor probably from the city called Methymna located on the Aegean island of Lesbos. The most important ancient building of Assos was the Temple of Athena, partly preserved to our times, standing on the acropolis of the city, overlooking the Aegean Sea.

In the 6th century BCE, Assos got under the rule of the kingdom of Lydia, and then shared the fate of this country, becoming a part of the Persian Empire. The satrap of this Persian province, called Ariobarzanes, joined the so-called Great Satraps' Revolt. Persian governors of the provinces, despite the support obtained from the Egyptian Pharaoh, the king of Sparta, and several Greek

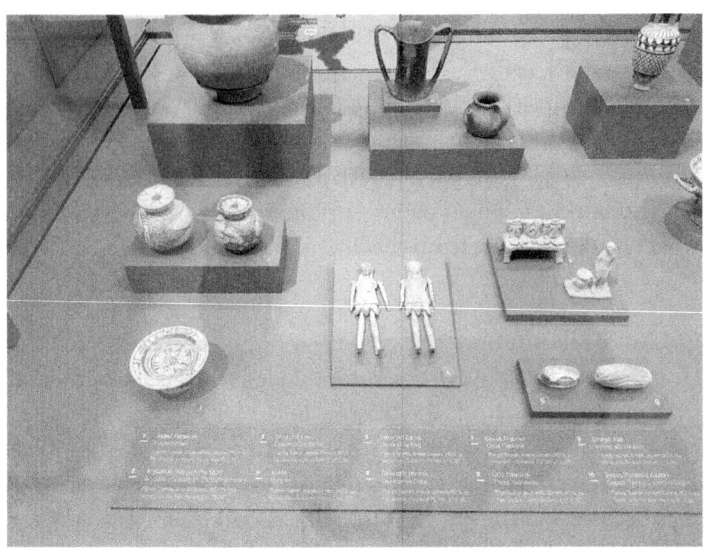

Finds from Assos

cities, suffered defeat at the Battle of Assos in 365 BCE.

The first archaeological excavations in Assos were conducted by the expedition of the American Archaeological Institute under the direction of J.T. Clarke and F.H. Bacon in the years 1881-1883. During the works, the scholars examined and documented the Temple of Athena, a gymnasium, an agora, a theatre, a bouleuterion, and the tombs in the necropolis. Under the mutual agreement, 2/3 of the exhibits were given to the Sultan, and 1/3 – were taken to America. They are on display in the Museum of Fine Arts in Boston.

After a break of nearly one hundred years, in 1981, new research in Assos was started by Professor Ümit Serdaroğlu. For him, the study of Assos became life's work. When the scientist died in 2005, he was buried in Assos. Since 2006, the work has been headed by Dr Nusret Arslan from the University of Çanakkale.

Among the finds from the local necropolis, such as vessels and terracotta objects from the 5th and the 4th centuries BCE, there are fascinating figurines of musicians. Most likely, they were funeral gifts because they have been found in the sarcophagi. Perhaps there is a connection between them and the cult of the god Dionysus. The figurines depict musicians playing various instruments, including the lyre, the cithara, the drum, and the flute, as well as people dancing and singing. These finds provided vital information on the burial customs of that period of history. Beside the Greek finds, also the traces of Lydian, Persian, Roman, Byzantine, and Ottoman periods have been found in Assos.

Lampsakos

Some fascinating exhibits have been brought to the museum from Lapseki (ancient Lampsakos), strategically situated on the Asian shore of the Dardanelles in the northern Troad. The city was founded by the Greeks from Miletus and Phokaia in the 7th century BCE. They were attracted to the north of Asia Minor by extremely fertile lands in the area. In antiquity, the city also was famous for its excellent wine.

Under the Roman rule, Lampsakos played an important role. Together with Abydos, located further to the south, at Cape Nara, it exercised total control over the movement of trade through the Hellespont (the Dardanelles) in the direction of the Black Sea. These two settlements were located in one of the narrowest points of this strait. Lampsakos also thrived in the Roman Imperial times and was favoured by Roman army veterans.

The most famous person connected with the history of Lampsakos is the renown natural philosopher Anaxagoras. He was born in Klazomenai – one of the cities of the Ionian League, but for most of his life he was a resident of Athens. His major work about nature has been preserved only in fragments, but it is known that Anaxagoras was the precursor of the scientific explanation of natural phenomena. Because of his views, belittling the role of the gods in the eyes of his contemporaries, he was prosecuted for impiety, and banished from Athens in 433 BCE. He spent the last years of his life in Lampsakos, where he was treated with great respect. After his death, an altar dedicated to the Spirit and the Truth was built in his honour in Lampsakos.

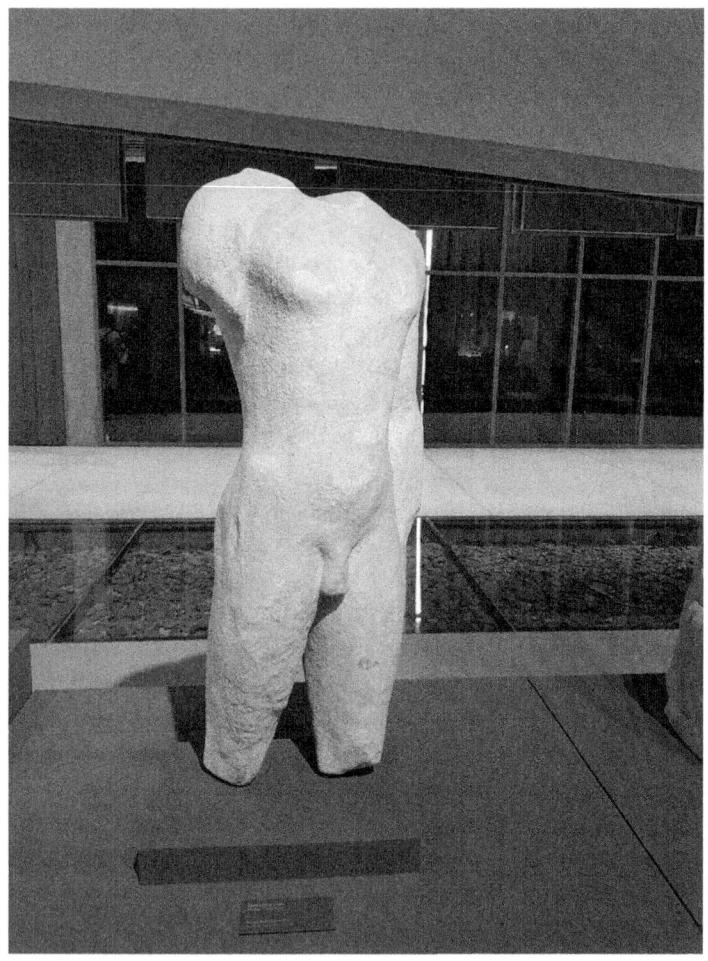

Kouros from Lampsakos

Other famous people associated with the city include: Anaximenes of Lampsacus – a historian, an orator, a pupil of Diogenes, and the teacher of Alexander the Great; Metrodoros of Lampsakos – a philosopher and a student of Epicurus; and another Metrodoros of Lampsakos – a philosopher, a student of Anaxagoras, and a commentator on Homer.

The finds from Lampaskos displayed in the Troy Museum are represented by a stone table leg and a statue of a young man called (so-called kouros) from the 6th century BCE. Particularly striking is the statue of the goddess Aphrodite from the Hellenistic period.

Alexandria Troas

Another archaeological site represented at the museum is Alexandria Troas, located on the shore of the Aegean Sea, opposite the island of Tenedos. The settlement in the area of Alexandria Troas had already existed before the Hellenistic period, and it was called Sigeia (Sigia). One of the generals of Alexander the Great, Antigonus I Monophthalmus, contributed to its development, through the resettlement of the residents of the surrounding towns around 310 BCE.

With time, Alexandria Troas became the most important port city in the north-western part of Asia Minor, as well as the wealthiest city of the Troad. It owed its spectacular development to its strategic position, on the Aegean coast near the entrance to the Dardanelles. It meant that Alexandria was a convenient harbour for the transit of goods transported on the route from the east to the port of Neapolis in Macedonia, and further – to Rome.

In Roman times, Alexandria Troas acquired the status of a free and autonomous city. It is estimated that it had a population of 100,000 people in the days of its greatest prosperity. Successive Roman emperors, including Augustus and Hadrian, contributed to the development of the city.

A famous Roman statesman, philosopher and man of substance – Herodes Atticus – was appointed by Emperor Hadrian to the position of prefect of the free cities of Asia, in 125 CE. While holding this title, he funded the aqueduct of Alexandria Troas,

Finds from Alexandria Troas

fragments of which have been preserved to our times. Herodes Atticus was also a sponsor of a local theatre and baths.

Emperor Constantine the Great had an intention of making Alexandria Troas the new capital of the empire, but in the end, his choice fell to Byzantium, later known as Constantinople. It is not known precisely when the city was abandoned, but with the growing importance of Constantinople, Alexandria Troas lost its leading position in the region.

In 267 CE, the Goths sacked the city, which had a substantial negative impact on its economic situation. It is known that over time the port was silted up, and the town fell into disrepair. In medieval times, travellers who saw the remains of Alexandria from the sea suspected that these had been the ruins of the legendary Troy and that they had seen the palace of the Trojan king Priam.

The site of Alexandria Troas was first excavated in 1993, and the work is continued today. The finds from this site displayed in the museum include terracotta figurines, lamps, pottery fragments, and coins. The statuettes of Kybele and Eros are prominent examples of the finds from Alexandria.

Among the most impressive exhibits, there is a marble lion statue from the 2nd century CE. The table leg in the shape of a lion's head from the 1st century CE also draws much attention because of its detailed design. Rare bronze finds are represented by a hand fragment of a statue and a furniture element from the 2nd century CE.

Apollon Smintheion

Apollon Smintheion sanctuary is located 47 kilometres to the south of Troy, on the shore of the Aegean Sea, near the village of Gülpinar. The temple was dedicated to Apollo Smintheus, often interpreted as the Lord of Mice. Why did one of the gods of the Greek pantheon earn the nickname associated with rodents, and why was his temple built in the Troad? There is no clear answer to these questions, but when searching for them, it is necessary to start from the source, that is, from Homer. The history of Apollo as the Lord of Mice began with the following fragment of the Iliad:

> *Not a word he spoke, but went by the shore of the sounding sea and prayed apart to King Apollo whom lovely Leto had borne.*
> *'Hear me,' he cried, 'O god of the silver bow, that protectest Chryse and holy Cilla and rulest Tenedos with thy might, hear me oh thou of Sminthe. If I have ever decked your temple with garlands, or burned your thigh-bones in fat of bulls or goats, grant my prayer, and let your arrows avenge these my tears upon the Danaans.'*
> Homer, the Iliad, Book I, translated by Samuel Butler

With these words, the priest of Apollo, Chryses, begs the god to bring revenge on the Greeks. Their main commander, Agamemnon, abducted his daughter, Chryseis. Apollo listened to this request, sent the plague onto the Greek army, and Chryseis was returned to her father. This situation became a source of conflict between Agamemnon and Achilles, the main theme of the Iliad.

The most enigmatic word in the quoted passage is the nickname

'Sminthe', given by Chryses to Apollo. The ancient Greeks had already found this word incomprehensible and attributed its origins to one of the Anatolian languages. Modern linguists agree with this opinion and derive the word from the Luvian language. Unfortunately, the epic poem of Homer does not provide any hints at the meaning of this word. Therefore, subsequent myths of Apollo tried to explain this nickname on the basis of the context in which it had been used in The Iliad. Since Apollo sent the plague on the Greeks, he was associated with rodents as major disease carriers. Therefore, Apollo, as the god that could send or finish an epidemic, became the 'Lord of Mice'.

The first archaeological excavations at the Temple of Apollo were carried out by the English architect Richard Popplewell Pullan. He received funding for the work at Teos, Priene, and the Temple of Apollon Smintheion, in the years 1863-1869.

Systematic excavations were later conducted in the temple in the period 1971-1973, under the auspices of the Archaeological Museum of Çanakkale. Since 1980, ongoing excavations have been undertaken by a team from the University of Ankara, under the leadership of Professor Coşkun Özgünel. The finds from these excavations are now on display in the Troy Museum. They include pottery and clay lamps as well as numerous glass bottles.

Moreover, the history of this site goes back as far as the Chalcolithic period, around 5000 BCE. Professor Turan Takaoğlu conducted the excavations of this layer. His team found the evidence of animal husbandry, fishing, hunting, and gathering of mussels and oysters. The early finds from Gülpinar displayed in the Troy Museum include well-burnished, dark-coloured pottery, cheese pots and strainers, and fascinating terracotta figurines with no mouths.

Çingenetepe Tumulus

Among the most prominent exhibits on the lowest level of the Troy Museum are the finds from the area known as Hellespontine Phrygia, situated around the Granicus and Aesepus Rivers. This region abounds in ancient tumuli, the huge artificial burial hills

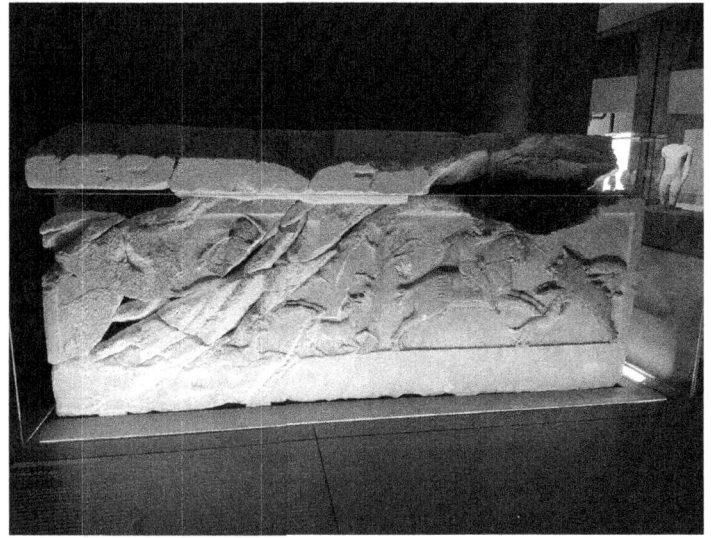

Altıkulaç Sarcophagus

that date back to the period between the second half of the 6th century and the first half of the 4th century BCE. Thus, these tumuli are from the times when the Persians dominated in the Troad.

These tumuli were the tombs of wealthy landowners affiliated with the satrapal capital of Dascylium, that lay about 70 kilometres to the east of the Granicus River. The magnificent tombs represented the aristocratic competition among the Anatolian elite: the greater was the number and size of the tumuli on an estate, the higher was the associated status of the family. To be more visible, these tombs were located in prominent places, such as on high ridges or near the major waterways. The level of wealth of the people buried in these tumuli is attested by both the tomb structures and the associated grave gifts.

One of the most impressive objects displayed on the lowest level of the museum is the so-called Altıkulaç Sarcophagus. It was found within the Çingenetepe Tumulus in a circular corbel-vaulted tomb in the village of Altıkulaç. This village is located near the town

Altıkulaç Sarcophagus

of Çan in the eastern Troad, in the Granicus River valley. The sarcophagus is, most probably, from the first quarter of the 4th century BCE, when the region was under the Persian control.

Two sides of the painted marble sarcophagus of Greco-Persian type are decorated with figural representations, and much of the original colours have been preserved. The front shows two different scenes: a boar hunt at the right and a fallow buck hunt at the left, while a leafless tree in the centre serves as a divider. The left part of this side is of particular interest as the figure of a hunter was chiselled off after the sarcophagus was finished and painted. This could indicate that the depicted person committed an offence against the family of the deceased.

On the short side, an Anatolian dynast from the Hellespontine Phrygia is depicted in hunting and battle scenes. The battle scene shows a mounted, armoured warrior, accompanied by his henchman, spearing a fallen light-armed soldier. The clothes of both figures suggest that it was a battle between a Greek and a Persian. The rider was almost certainly the dynast to whom the sarcophagus belonged while the henchman, judging from his appearance, was probably a Greek mercenary in the service of the cavalryman.

The skeletal remains that were found in the sarcophagus belong to the man in his twenties. He must have suffered severe injuries, either in battle or after falling off a horse when many of his limbs had been crushed. He lived for several more years as a cripple, his limbs remaining misaligned. As his bones did not heal properly, he experienced pain for the rest of his life.

Dedetepe Tumulus

Dedetepe Tumulus, also situated in the Granicus Plain, dates back to the early 5th century BCE. It was excavated in 1994 by the archaeologists from Çanakkale Archaeological Museum. It contains a burial chamber measuring 3.60 by 3.60 meters, erected of marble blocks connected with lead clamps, preceded by an antechamber. Inside the chamber, there were two marble banqueting couches called klinai, placed respectively against the rear wall and the left wall. They had painted decoration with palmettes, volutes and meander patterns, in yellow, red, blue, green, and black. In front of the couches, there were elaborately decorated wooden stools. As four skulls were discovered within the chamber, it is assumed that it had been used for several generations.

The chamber had been robbed, not only once but twice, for the first time in the Hellenistic times. Interestingly, the ancient robbers left their traces in the form of the sweat and mud marks on the walls and the couches. Possibly, they attempted to clean their hands during the act of robbery. Despite the plunder, the archaeologists found some fragments of wooden furniture and an ivory knife handle in the shape of a stag head.

Moreover, alabaster vessels and pieces of musical instruments were recovered, indicating that a meal was held there during the funeral celebrations. The exhibition in the Troy Museum recreates the interior of the grave chamber. The multimedia demonstration shows how it had originally appeared.

Recreated interior of Dedetepe Tumulus

Parion

Parion was a Greek city located on the border of historical lands of Troad and Mysia. In ancient times, Parion functioned as an important harbour for the surrounding settlements. The origin of the town's name has not yet been scientifically explained, but there is a tradition that it comes from Paris, the son of the Trojan king Priam.

The city was founded probably about 3,000 years ago as a colony by settlers from Eretria (a Greek polis from the island of Euboea), Miletus, and the island of Paros in the Aegean Sea. Parion was a member of the Delian League. In the city, there were defensive towers, and at least four temples.

In the Hellenistic period, it came under the control of Lysimachus – one of diadochi of Alexander the Great. After his death, the city was taken over by the Attalids from Pergamon. As a part of the Pergamon Kingdom, Parion was handed over to the Romans by the will of Attalos III in 133 BCE.

Antique coins from Parion testify to its great importance and

Finds from Parion

advanced minting facilities. The most interesting picture, visible on the coins from the Hellenistic period, is the coat of arms. It depicts the so-called gorgoneion, i.e. the head of the Gorgon – a terrible mythological beast with sharp fangs, and hair in the form of poisonous snakes. In ancient times, gorgoneion served as an apotropaic amulet, reversing evil charms. Similar role is now played by nazar boncuğu – a popular Turkish amulet. The relation between the city of Parion and the Gorgon is not fully understood, most likely the monster was chosen as the emblem of the city to reverse bad intentions and repel attacks against its inhabitants. Perhaps it had to do with military power represented by Parion.

Archaeological work has been conducted at the ruins of Parion for many years. The existence of ancient Parion was no secret to the father of the Turkish archaeology – Osman Hamdi Bey. He found a sarcophagus there, later transported to the Archaeological Museum in Istanbul.

From 2005 to 2015, a team of archaeologists in Parion was directed by Professor Cevat Başaran from Atatürk University in

Erzurum. The current director of the works is Professor Vedat Keleş.

The most important discoveries made by the team of archaeologists are tombs and sarcophagi from the area of Parion necropolis. Among them, it is worth mentioning a 2200-year-old sarcophagus, which was unearthed in 2009. Golden earrings found in it bear the symbol of Eros, and they were accompanied by numerous rings and some fragments of the crown decorated with precious stones. These finds allow the presumption that a rich person was buried there, and she was called the princess of Parion by the discoverers of the tomb.

Unfortunately, the bones of the people buried in the necropolis have not been well preserved because of soil moisture due to the proximity of the sea. A royal crown and gold coins with the figure of the sun god were discovered in another tomb.

In addition to these special sarcophagi, around 200 graves have been discovered in the necropolis so far, often with gifts for the dead, including bottles for tears, oil lamps, and toys. Sometimes the funeral gifts enable the identification of the occupation of the person buried there, as in the case of the tomb with bronze fragments of a fishing rod from the 1st century CE.

Among the finds from Parion displayed in the Troy Museum, the most beautiful artefact is a decorated bronze amphora found in 2005. It probably dates back to the second half of the 4th century BCE, but its current state is the result of the restoration carried out in 2010. Other artefacts from Parion on display include the statue of Orpheus from the end of the first century BCE and numerous clay lamps and vessels.

Pegaea

The ancient city of Pegaea was located on the plain of Adrastea, which is the borderland between the historical lands of Troad and Mysia. The main event that is linked with the history of Pegea happened on the banks of a small river flowing through the city. It is now known as Biga Çayı, although there are also two other names – Çan Çayı and Kocabaş Çayı. This river, flowing from the northern slopes of the massif of Ida Mountain, meets the Sea of Marmara after negotiating 80 km through the area of the Troad. It is best known by its ancient name – Granicus River. In May of 334 BCE, in the Battle of the Granicus, very near Pegea, the army of Alexander the Great defeated the Persian forces, opening the way for the Macedonians to the conquest of Asia Minor.

As no systematic archaeological work has been carried out, the oldest history of the human settlement remains a mystery to researchers. Nowadays, the city is called Biga, and it is now the largest city in the central part of the Troad. Pegaea is represented in the Troy Museum by a marble tombstone from the 2nd century CE.

Gallipoli Peninsula

The museum also has among its collections the items found in archaeological sites located on the Gallipoli Peninsula. The sculpture of a horse from the 4th century CE has come from Lysimacheia (near Bolayır), and the gravestone of an athlete from the 5th century BCE has been found in the vicinity of Küçükanafarta (near Eceabat).

Neolithic settlements of the Troad

The first settlements in the region of Troad, reaching back to the Neolithic period, i.e. 8000 BCE, are also represented in the Troy Museum. The first of them is known as Coşkuntepe (Bademli), located in the south-western corner of the Troad. This significant Neolithic settlement was situated on a natural hill over the coast. The excavations suggested that the earliest inhabitants of this site lived around 6000 BCE, and they made their living through fishing and animal husbandry.

Another settlement of this period is Hanaytepe (Bozköy), near Ezine, 13 kilometres to the south of Troy. This tumulus is considered as one of the most important prehistoric settlement areas of the region. It was first studied by professor Rüstem Aslan, the current head of the Troy excavations. He stated that this is the second biggest tumulus of the Troad after Troy. The essential finds include high-quality stone-headed hand axes made around 3000 BCE.

Alacaligöl site is located around four kilometres to the west of Troy. Some researchers speculate that this low-lying area was a convenient harbour location for Troy. The excavations conducted since the year 2000 have revealed the existence of a prehistoric settlement site, dated to the Neolithic and Chalcolithic periods.

Beşik-Sivritepe tumulus is among the most famous one from the Troad region. For a long time, it has been believed to be a monumental grave of one of the heroes of the Trojan War, possibly Achilles himself, and thus it has been dubbed the Achilleion. It was first excavated at the end of the 19th century by Heinrich Schliemann, who used there the same drastic measures that he applied at Troy. He dug a tunnel to enter the burial chamber. Due to the extensive excavations carried out on top of the tumulus, the layers were largely destroyed, so the proper stratification became impossible.

More recently, Manfred Korfmann, the long-time director of Troy excavations, also studied the tumulus, from 1983 to 1987. The finds from Beşik-Sivritepe include pottery sherds collected by Schliemann: they represent hand-made, brown, black and yellow burnished ware. Moreover, the abundance of oysters and mussel shells discovered at this site suggests that these sea animals were an essential source of food. The location was inhabited between 4800 and 4000 BCE.

Trojan Treasure

Finally, the lowest floor exhibition also displays the so-called Trojan Treasure. Some of the golden objects on display were previously in the collections of the Istanbul Archaeological Museum. The significant group of artefacts was returned to Turkey in 2012 from the University of Pennsylvania Museum of Archaeology and Anthropology. This institution acquired these fantastic pieces of gold jewellery in 1966. When the scientific analyses indicated that these objects had come from Troy, the treasure was transferred back to Turkey, thanks to the efforts of the Turkish Ministry of Culture.

Troy Museum

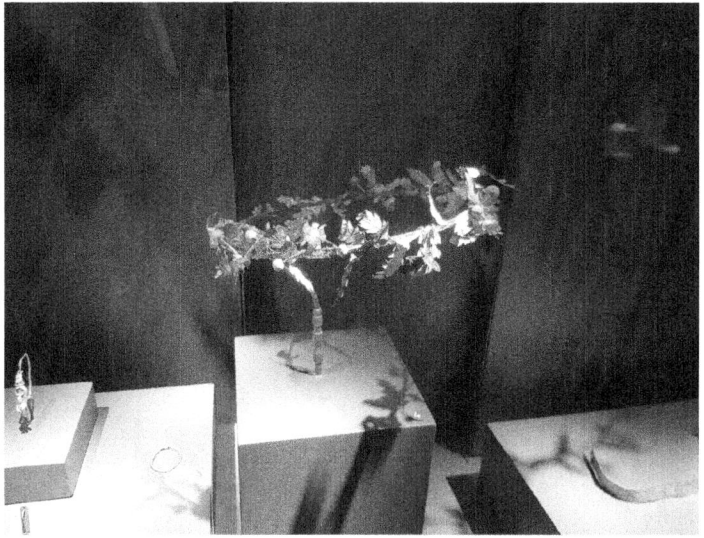

Trojan Treasure exhibition

Level 1 – Layers of Troy

The ramp takes the visitors to the second level of the museum. Along the ramp, the introduction of bronze as a new kind of metal is presented, and the history of Early Bronze Age Asia Minor is discussed. Moreover, the neighbours of Troy from the northern Aegean islands, Western Anatolia, and Thrace are introduced.

The exhibition on the second level of the museum is dedicated to the explanation of the layers of the archaeological site of Troy. The exhibits from the layers of Troy have been grouped into six categories, representing Troy I, II, III, IV-V, VI, and VII. These layers and development stages of Troy are described in chronological order, with Troy II, VI, and VII particularly prominent as the most prosperous stages of the ancient city.

There is a multimedia presentation that helps to understand the changes of Troy over the millennia. Moreover, the changing geography of the region is carefully explained, emphasising that when Troy was founded around 3000 BCE, it was located close to a deep lagoon. In time, the alluvium brought by the Scamander

Chronology of Troy

and Simoeis rivers gradually silted and filled this lagoon.

The exhibition on the second level also gets back to other settlements of the region, explaining their chronology in relation to the history of Troy. Therefore, apart from the artefacts from Troy, also the finds from other Neolithic settlements of the Troad are exhibited here, including the ones from Beşik-Sivritepe and Kumtepe.

Moreover, the exhibition presents and explains various aspects of daily life in ancient Troy, including masonry, weaving, pottery-making, and cooking methods. A particular emphasis is on the importance of Troy in the maritime trade in the Bronze Age.

The ancient art of weaving is demonstrated in the museum by a loom reconstructed on the basis of the fragments found by Carl Blegen inside a burned building. The fabric on display was woven using the replicas of loom weights, found in thousands within the ancient site of Troy. On display, there are also spindle whorls and the objects related to dye production and sewing.

The food production process of the Trojan Maritime Culture –

The oldest known painted vessel

Cooking Culture exhibition

i.e. the earliest three layers of Troy – is represented in the museum by numerous finds, including grinding stones, lids, plates, tripod vessels, bowls, and jugs. A red-painted jar found in 1995 and considered to be the oldest known painted vessel fragment is also on display.

The aesthetic aspects of the early Trojan's lives are also represented in the exhibition. On display, there are quartz objects such as a lion heart or a pendant. The gold jewellery collection includes a gold earring. An exciting exhibit is related to the process of jewellery production: a stone jewellery mould from the Middle Bronze Age.

The objects excavated from the layer of Troy II include the collections of plates, dishes decorated with spatial figures, and many drinking vessels, including the specimens of the so-called depas amphikypellon – a term used by Homer to describe high and narrow vessels with two handles, and the vessels similar in shape to modern mugs. The museum has exhibits from later chronological layers of Troy, including Troy V – dishes and pots, and Troy VI-

VIIa – Mycenaean vessels. There are also special thematic display cases devoted to weapons, bone tools, and bronze objects.

Level 2 – Ancient World

The wide ramp takes the visitors to the third level of the museum. As the guests climb to this level, they are introduced to the history of the transitional period between the Bronze Age and the Iron Age. Moreover, new civilizations that developed in Asia Minor between 1200 and 800 BCE are presented, including the Phrygians and the Lydians.

The exhibition of this level also offers insights into the realities of other cities of the Troad in the Roman period. The artefacts come from Alexandria Troas, a harbour city that controlled the maritime traffic in the area. A marble pedestal with the inscription mentioning Emperor Hadrian comes from Parion, a city declared as a privileged one by Augustus. Another exhibit – a marble inscription – was found in the city of Maydos, now Eceabat on the Gallipoli Peninsula.

The most prominent artefacts from the Roman-period Ilium are the sculptures documenting the importance of the city to Roman Emperors. The first one is the head of Emperor Augustus, found in Troy excavations. The most beautiful exhibit is the larger-than-life cuirassed statue of Emperor Hadrian found in the odeon of Troy.

Another fascinating exhibits are the terracotta plaques of a horseman, found as votive objects within Troy's Western Sanctuary. They depict a young, unbearded male rider wearing a cloak. A snake appears beneath his horse, indicating the cult of a hero. Professor Brian Rose suggested that this figure represents Dardanos, the mythical ancestor of the Trojans. His son, Ilus, was regarded as the founder of Troy, and the name of the city – Ilium/Ilios – came from him. Other finds from the Western Sanctuary are the figurines of Kybele, the mother-goddess, depicted with a lion on her lap and wearing a mural crown on her head.

One of the most striking artefacts displayed on this floor is the so-called Polyxena Sarcophagus from Kızöldün Tumulus. It is 2500

Inscription from Parion

Troy Museum

Statue of Emperor Hadrian found at Troy

years-old and would better fit into the exhibition at the lowest level of the museum. Its placement on the third level most probably results from the history that is narrated on its decorated sides.

Kızöldün Tumulus is the oldest known tumulus of Hellespontine Phrygia. It was found in the Granicus River valley, near Biga in the Province of Çanakkale in 1994. The discovery was the result of the rescue operations carried out after the authorities had been notified about illegal digs in the area. Within the tumulus, the archaeologists found two marble sarcophagi: one representing the sacrifice of Polyxena, dating to around 500-490 BCE, and another containing the body of a 10-year-old girl, buried 40 or 50 years later.

Polyxena Sarcophagus is a remarkable object as it is one of the earliest stone sarcophagi with figural scenes ever to have been found in Asia Minor. It represents the early example of the Proconnesian marble workshops. It has impressive dimensions of 3.32 meters in length, 1.60 meters in width, and 1.78 meters in height. A whole in the cover of the sarcophagus indicates that it had been robbed in antiquity. Moreover, fragments of a wheeled cart that transported the corpse to the tumulus were discovered beneath the terracotta tiles that surrounded the sarcophagus. Although the figures of the reliefs depict mainly women, the person buried was a 40-year-old man.

The reliefs on the sarcophagus show a funerary celebration on three sides, and on the back what is believed to be the sacrifice of Polyxena by Neuptolemos in front of the tomb of his father Achilles. Although not mentioned by Homer, Polyxena was a well-known figure of Greek mythology.

Polyxena was the youngest daughter of King Priam of Troy and his wife, Hecuba. An oracle prophesied that Troy would not be defeated if Polyxena's brother, Prince Troilus, reached the age of twenty. The siblings were ambushed when they were attempting to fetch water from a fountain, and Troilus was killed by Achilles, who soon became interested in Polyxena. He seemed to trust Polyxena, and he told her of his only vulnerability: his heel.

Troy Museum

Polyxena Sarcophagus

Polyxena revealed this secret to her brothers, Paris and Deiphobus, who ambushed Achilles and shot him in the heel with an arrow. At the end of the Trojan War, Achilles' ghost came back to the Greeks to demand the human sacrifice of Polyxena to appease the wind needed to set sail back to Greece. She was to be killed at the foot of Achilles' grave. Polyxena was eager to die as a sacrifice to Achilles rather than live as a slave. She refused to beg for mercy and died bravely as the son of Achilles, Neoptolemus, slit her throat.

The second sarcophagus found in the same location, is just over half the size of the first. It contained the skeleton of a girl aged between eight and ten. Luckily, this sarcophagus had not been plundered, and it stored a group of burial gifts including gold boat-shaped earrings, two elaborate necklaces, bracelets with antelope-head terminals, a silver ladle and plate, baked clay alabaster vessels, a glass aryballos, and a painted wooden female figurine. Many of these objects have been influenced by the Achaemenid style dominant at the time in the region, and this also applies to the architectural decoration of the sarcophagus.

Trojan War geographic model

Finally, this floor of the museum boasts a huge model of the Trojan War based on the geography of the region. It shows Greek armies and ships in a bay as well as the city of King Priam with its houses and the inner fortress. The narrative of the Trojan War is supported by a multimedia presentation of the friezes from Apollon Smintheion Temple. There, the scenes from Homer's Iliad are presented in bas-relief. A map shows the main characters of the Trojan War, both on the Greek and the Trojan sides, placing them into a geographical context of the region. This part of the exhibition is supplemented with classical Greek vessels with the depictions of the scenes from the Trojan War.

Level 3 – Troy Excavations History

The ramp to the highest level of the exhibition presents the latest history of Troy. The information boards explain how the location of Troy was forgotten, but its heritage was not. It emphasises how many European dynasties regarded themselves as the descendants of the Trojans, including the Franks, the Venetians, and the Habs-

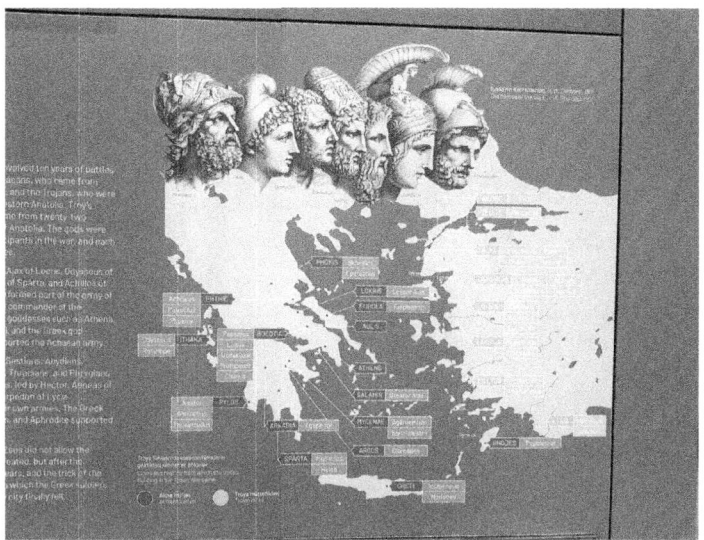

Heroes of the Trojan War

burgs. Along the ramp, there are also reprints of the old maps that tried to pinpoint the exact location of Troy.

Moreover, the links between the Ottomans and Troy are explained, starting from Sultan Mehmed the Conqueror who claimed that he had avenged Troy by conquering Constantinople. His sentiments were repeated much later, by the first president of the Turkish Republic, Mustafa Kemal Atatürk. In 1922, after the victory over the Greek army, he stated that 'at Dumlupınar, we avenged Hector'.

The exhibitions on the highest level of the museum are divided into several categories, including the history of Troy excavations, Troy in the Gallipoli battles, Troy in popular culture and art, but also Ottoman Çanakkale and the Lost Heritage.

The history of Troy excavations is the central part of this exhibition. It has a form of crates filled with archaeological finds, mainly pottery fragments, surrounded by the information boards about the archaeological exploration of the site. This installation is completed with the photographs from the excavation site.

The Secrets of Troy

Troy Excavations History exhibition

The main aim of the exhibit, besides providing basic information, is the demonstration how Troy has become one of the most important reference points for the archaeological exploration of the Aegean region. It also demonstrates that Troy is the site where modern archaeology was born. Much attention is paid to the archaeologists who worked at Troy: Frank Calvert, Heinrich Schliemann, Wilhelm Dörpfeld, Carl W. Blegen, and Manfred Osman Korfmann.

The Lost Heritage section is devoted to the artefacts that had been taken out of the country by Heinrich Schliemann who smuggled many finds out of the Ottoman Empire. Despite his excavation permit that required that he shared the finds 50-50 with the Ottoman government, Schliemann smuggled most of the so-called Priam Treasure to Greece, via the harbour at Kumkale. Today, the major part of this treasure is in Russia, in the Pushkin Museum in Moscow and the Hermitage in St. Petersburg. The special multimedia presentation enables the visitors of the Troy Museum to see some of these lost artefacts.

Troy Museum

Ottoman Çanakkale exhibition

Ottoman Çanakkale exhibition displays old engravings depicting this city. There are also some examples of the famous Çanakkale ceramics as well as the Ottoman-period tombstones, architectural fragments, and coins. The importance of the Ottoman settlements and the Dardanelles in the early days of the Ottoman Empire are also discussed.

Visitor tips for Troy Museum

Troy Museum is situated 700 meters to the east of Troy archaeological site. The visiting hours are 8:30 am to 7:00 pm from 1 April to 31 October, and 8:30 am to 5:30 pm from 1 November to 31 March. The ticket office closes half an hour earlier. The museum is closed until 1 pm on the first day of religious holidays.

The ticket to the museum costs 42 TL. Children below 8 enter for free. There is also a possibility to purchase a combined ticket to Troy and the nearby Troy Museum for 60 TL.

The Secrets of Troy

Bibliography

1. Aşkın, M., *Troy. A Revised Edition*, Istanbul, 2001
2. Aslan, C. C., C. B. Rose. *City and citadel at Troy from the Late Bronze Age through the Roman period*. in: Cities and Citadels in Turkey: from the Iron Age to the Seljuks, 2013
3. Aslan, C. C. *Swan imagery at the West Sanctuary at Troia*, in: SOMA 2007. Proceedings of the XI Symposium on Mediterranean Archaeology, Istanbul Technical University, 24-29 April 2007
4. Ceram, C.W., *Gods, Graves & Scholars: The Story of Archaeology*, 1986
5. Constantinescu, D., and B. A. Carlan. *Heritage concerning the usage of water resources in the defence sites of ancient Roman Empire*, International Journal of Heritage Architecture 1.4 (2017): 704-712
6. Erbil, Y., and Alice Mouton. *Water in ancient Anatolian religions: an archaeological and philological inquiry on the Hittite evidence*, Journal of Near Eastern Studies 71.1 (2012): 53-74
7. Gordon, E. *The Meaning of the Ideogram dKASKAL. KUR = 'Underground Water-Course' and its Significance for Bronze Age Historical Geography*, Journal of Cuneiform Studies 21.1 (1967): 70-88
8. Jablonka, P., and C. Brian Rose. *Late Bronze Age Troy: A Response to Frank Kolb*, American Journal of Archaeology, 108.4 (2004): 615-630
9. Kayan, I., *Kesik plain and Alacaligöl mound an assessment of the Paleogeography around Troia*, Studia Troica, 18 (2009): 105-128.

10. Korfmann, M., *Troia/Wilusa. Guidebook*, Çanakkale, 2005
11. Riorden, E. *A Hadrianic Theater at Ilion (Troy): a Paradigm Shift for Roman Building Practice and Its Aesthetic Aftermath*, in: Proceedings of the Second International Congress on Construction History, Volume 3, 2006
12. Rose, C. B., and R. Körpe, *The Tumuli of Troy and the Troad*, in: Tumulus as Sema, Space, Politics, Culture and Religion in the First Millennium BC, Berlin/Boston, 2016
13. Tolstikov, V., and Treister, Mikhail, *The Gold of Troy. Searching for Homer's Fabled City*, London, 1996
14. Traill, D., *Schliemann of Troy: Treasure and Deceit*, New York, 1997
15. Troy Culture Route, https://www.troycultureroute.com/, accessed: December 2019

About the Author

IZABELA MISZCZAK is the editor of TurkishArchaeoNews.net website devoted to the cultural heritage of Asia Minor. She holds a master diploma in social sciences from the Faculty of Social Sciences, the University of Silesia in Katowice, Poland, with the specialization in the sociology of culture. She has authored several publications in the area of political studies and social sciences. She has written several guidebooks in Polish and English. She is also the editor of TurcjaWSandalach.pl portal for independent travellers. She lives in Poland with her husband, two kids, and two dogs.

About Turkish Archaeological News

TAN stands for Turkish Archaeological News, a website

https://TurkishArchaeoNews.net/

created in 2013 with the aim of providing news about the latest archaeological discoveries in Turkey and neighbouring regions. The project has been developed into a travel portal, dedicated to history buffs who visit Turkey searching for historical buildings, ancient ruins, and fascinating museums. TAN website publishes texts about such places as well as the news concerning archaeological excavations and discoveries. All our texts are illustrated with original photos that TAN editorial team has taken during our travels around Turkey. We have been visiting this beautiful country regularly since 2004, and the website, as well as TAN Travel Guides, are the reflection of our ongoing fascination with Asia Minor.

Printed in Great Britain
by Amazon